ROYAL COURT THEATRE PRESENTS

Bodies

by Vivienne Franzmann

les was first performed at the Royal Court Jerwood
tre Upstairs, Sloane Square, on Wednesday 5 July 2017.

Bodies

by Vivienne Franzmann

CAST (in alphabetical order)

Oni **Lorna Brown**
Josh **Brian Ferguson**
David **Philip Goldacre**
Lakshmi **Salma Hoque**
Clem **Justine Mitchell**
Daughter **Hannah Rae**
Dr Sharma (voice only) **Manjinder Virk**
Boy **Alexander Molony, Rohan Shinn**

Director **Jude Christian**
Designer **Gabriella Slade**
Lighting & Projection Designer **Joshua Pharo**
Sound Designer **Helen Skiera**
Film Maker **Meghna Gupta**
Director of Photography **Susie Salavati**
Casting Director **Amy Ball**
Production Manager **Marty Moore**
Costume Supervisor **Lydia Cawson**
Stage Managers **Nic Donithorn, Tamsin Withers**
Chaperone **Chelsea Smith**
Set Built by **Set Blue Scenery**

The Royal Court would like to thank the following for their help with this producti
Anaya Ballam, Esther Branch, Jan Clarke, Jess Gow, Meg Kubota, Deirdre Mah
Vinay Patel, Radisson Blu Edwardian Vanderbilt Hotel, Kat Tippins. And Sudha
Bhuchar for Hindi translation and dialect coaching.

Bodies

Vivienne Franzmann

vienne Franzmann (Writer)

the Royal Court: **Pests (& Clean Break), The
.ness.**

er theatre includes: **Mogadishu (Royal Exchange,
nchester/Lyric, Hammersmith/National
r), The Snow Queen (Bristol Old Vic).**

vision includes: **Colour, Lizard Girl.**

io includes: **Mogadishu, Ink Deep, The Witness**

rds include: **2008 Bruntwood Prize for
ywriting (Mogadishu); 2010 George Devine
ard (Mogadishu); 2012 Pearson Bursary
e Witness); 2014 BAFTA Award for Children's
rning - Primary Category (Lizard Girl).**

rna Brown (Oni)

the Royal Court: **Torn, Clybourne Park, 93.2FM.**

er theatre includes: **Oresteia (Almeida/West
); Little Light (Orange Tree); Medea,
rred Lines, Damned by Despair, The Cry of
Cricket (National); Crowning Glory, The
Life, Da Boyz, Funny Black Women on the
e, Shoot to Win, One Dance Will Do (Theatre
al, Stratford East); Fear (Bush); Short Fuses
stol Old Vic); Once on this Island (Hackney
pire/National tour); Things of Dry Hours
yal Exchange, Manchester/Gate); trade
C); The Hommage Behind (West End); Mass
ib, Zumbi (UK tour); The Weave (Soho); Anasi
als (Talawa); Up Against the Wall (Tricycle);
ello (New Vic); Once on This Island (West
/Birmingham Rep).**

vision includes: **Chewing Gum, Holby City, True
e, Outnumbered, Catherine Tate, Doctors,
Bill, The Vivienne Vyle Show, The Ronnie
:ona Show, Much Ado About Nothing, French
aunders, Family Business, Rough Treatment,
Girls, Casualty, Anna Lee.**

includes: **The Lady in the Van, Taking Stock,
Miserables, World War Z, Gambit, Little
lier.**

de Christian (Director)

irector, for the Royal Court: **Lela & Co.**

irector, other theatre includes: **The Path
ghtide); Blue (RWCMD); Split/Mixed
mmerhall); How Do You Eat An Elephant/
rta Eliffant, Sut Mae Gwneud Hynny
edwch? (National Youth Theatre of Wales);
py, The Mushroom (Pentabus Young
ters' Festival); Punk Rock, Last Easter
DA); I'd Rather Goya Robbed Me of My Sleep
n Some Other Arsehole (Gate/Boom Arts);
ansera (Poole Lighthouse); Sonata
ements (Blue Elephant).**

As writer/performer, theatre includes: **Nanjing (The
Yard).**

As director, opera includes: **©alculated to Death
(Tête-à-Tête Festival), Hidden in Plain Sight
(Académie du Festival d'Aix-en-Provence).**

As Associate Director, theatre includes: **The Darkest
Corners (Transform); Shopping & Fucking,
Aladdin (Lyric Hammersmith); Carmen
Disruption (Almeida).**

Jude is an Associate Artist at The Yard Theatre,
the Gate Theatre and the Lyric Hammersmith.

Brian Ferguson (Josh)

For the Royal Court: **Adler & Gibb.**

Other theatre includes: **A Number (Lyceum,
Edinburgh); Oil (Almeida); Anything That
Gives Off Light (& The TEAM), Rupture, Snuff,
Black Watch (National Theatre of Scotland);
The Broken Heart, The Changeling (Globe);
Hamlet, Observe the Sons of Ulster ... (Citizens,
Glasgow); Threeway (Edinburgh Festival Fringe/
Invisible Dot); The Game Show (Bush); The Aztec
Trilogy, Richard III, Dunsinane, Shakespeare
in a Suitcase (RSC); Money (Arches, Glasgow);
Earthquakes in London (National); The Guard,
Fall, The Dark Things (Traverse); The Drawer
Boy, Love Freaks (Tron); Bridgebuilders, Falling
(Poorboy).**

Television includes: **Trust Me, Kiss Me First, Line of
Duty, Our World War, Taggart, River City, The
Prayer, Doctors, Field of Blood.**

Film includes: **The Current War, Beats, Imagine
That, King, Residue, Voices, The Woods.**

Philip Goldacre (David)

Theatre includes: **The Reappearance of Christ
in the East End (White Bear); Broken
Glass (National/West End/UK tour); Great
Expectations (Birmingham Rep/Churchill,
Bromley); Relatively Speaking (Edinburgh
Festival Fringe/UK tour); West (Donmar);
Othello (Shaw); St John's Gospel (Riding Lights/
UK tour); Bruegel, Beryllium (Ragamuffin/
international tour); Chicken Soup with Barley
(New End); Cock Ups (Bridge Lane).**

Television includes: **The Canterbury Tales, The Bill,
Victoria & Albert, Out of This World, Michael
Winner's True Crimes, Brookside, Tucker's
Luck, The Tripods.**

Film includes: **The Journey of Alfred Small, Boy
& Wolf, Snowman, Tomb Raider: Ascension,
Wednesday, The Vision.**

Meghna Gupta (Film Maker)

As director, film includes: **Off the Grid.**

As producer, film includes: **Nasty.**

Meghna Gupta is a director whose work is characterised by a cinematic and intimate approach, often touching on the lives of women. Her debut, Unravel, screened at over 60 festivals and won over 20 awards, including an Al Jazeera Jury Award. She directs and produces film for the festival circuit as well as for the education and third sector.

Salma Hoque (Lakshmi)

Theatre includes: **East is East (ATG/UK tour); Multitudes (Tricycle); Drawing the Line (Hampstead).**

Television includes: **Doctors, Fam, Holby City.**

Justine Mitchell (Clem)

For the Royal Court: **Gastronauts, The Stone.**

Other theatre includes: **The Resistible Rise of Arturo Ui, King Lear (Donmar); Wild Honey (Hampstead); The Plough & the Stars, Detroit, Children of the Sun, The White Guard, The Hour We Knew Nothing of Each Other, Philistines, The Coram Boy, The House of Bernada Alba, Night Season (National); For Services Rendered (Chichester Festival); Love for Love, Twelfth Night (RSC); Man – Three Plays by Tennessee Williams, Uncle Vanya (Young Vic); The Rivals (Arcola); Mr Burns (Almeida); Nocturnal (Gate); Boston Marriage, Hedda Gabler, Footfalls, Pride & Prejudice, Blithe Spirit, Bash (Gate, Dublin); Three Sisters, Aristocrats, Shape of Metal, She Stoops to Conquer, The House of Bernarda Alba, All My Sons (Abbey, Dublin); The Way of All Flesh (Bewley's Dublin); A Midsummer Night's Dream (Nottingham Playhouse); A Streetcar Named Desire, The Importance of Being Earnest, Hayfever, A Voyage Round My Father (Pitlochry); A Christmas Carol (Communicado); This Misanthrope (Borderline).**

Television includes: **The Suspicions of Mr Whicher, Harry & Paul, Amber, Afterlife, Doctors, Joyball, New Tricks, Psych Ward, Sleep with Me, The Painted Lady, Waking the Dead, Wild at Heart, Your Bad Self.**

Film includes: **The Stag, I Want Candy, A Cock & Bull Story, Imagine Me & You, Inside I'm Dancing, Citizen Verdict, The Honeymooners, Goldfish Memory, Conspiracy of Silence.**

Radio includes: **Regenerations, Seasons of Fear.**

Alexander Molony (Boy)

Bodies is Alexander's professional stage debut.

Joshua Pharo (Lighting & Projecti Designer)

Theatre includes: **The Shape of Pain (China Plate How My Light is Spent (Royal Exchange, Manchester); The Bear & the Proposal (Youn Vic); Scarlett (Hampstead/Theatr Clywd); Ye of Sunlight (503); The Twits (Curve, Leicester Removal Men (Yard); Burning Doors (Belarus Free Theatre); Broken Biscuits (Paines Ploug The Future (Company Three); Contractions (Crucible, Sheffield); Julie (Northern Stage); Giving (Hampstead); Iphigenia Quartet, in th Night Time, Medea, I'd Rather Goya Robbed Me of My Sleep Than Some Other Arsehole, No Place Like Home (Gate); The Rolling Stone (Orange Tree); The Glass Menagerie (Nuffield The Merchant of Venice, Wuthering Heights (West End); The Crocodile (Manchester International Festival); One Arm (Southwark Amadis de Gaulle (Bloomsbury); Beckett Season (Old Red Lion); The Deluge (Lila Danc UK tour); Usagi Yojimbo (Southwark); Pionee (Curious Detective/UK tour); Thumbelina (Dancing Brick/UK Tour).**

Hannah Rae (Daughter)

Theatre includes: **Great Expectations (Rose, Kingston); A Midsummer Night's Dream (Sta Sevenoaks); Limit to Your Love (Magic Beans Romeo4Juliet (MB Productions).**

Television includes: **Broadchurch.**

Film includes: **Fighting with My Family, City of Ti Lights.**

Hannah is currently training at Central Sch of Speech and Drama.

Susie Salavati (Director of Photography)

Feature Films include: **My Feral Heart!.**

Documentaries include: **Even When I Fall, Where i the World, Unravel, Off the Grid.**

Awards include: **Cinequest 2016 Audience Award for Best Feature Drama (My Feral Heart!); W LA Award for Best Cinematography (Unravel Special Mention in the Best Cinematographe category at London Underwire Film Festival (Twitcher).**

Susie is a London–based Director of Photography, with diverse experience shoot drama and documentary in a multitude of worldwide locations. Her documentary, Off the Grid, was selected for Aesthetica and Copenhagen International Documentary Festival. She is a contributor to Getty Image and a member of international and UK base cinematography collectives the ICFC and Illuminatrix.

Rohan Shinn (Boy)

Bodies is Rohan's professional stage debut.

elen Skiera (Sound Designer)

associate sound designer, for the Royal Court: **Adler Gibb.**

sound designer, other theatre includes: **Echo's End,** e Magna Carta Plays (Salisbury Playhouse); use and Garden (Watermill); Good Dog, now all the secrets in my world, The gend of Hamba, The Epic Adventure of amo the Manyika Warrior (Tiata Fahodzi/ tford Palace); Here I Belong (Pentabus); e Encounter (Complicite); Harajuku Girls nborough); The Dog the Night & the Knife, ndora's Box, Miss Julie (Arcola); The Boy Who mbed Out of His Face (Shunt); Last Words u'll Hear (Almeida); I'd Rather Goya Robbed of My Sleep Than Some Other Arsehole ite, as Associate); Advice for the Young at art (Theatre Centre), Once In A Lifetime, e Eighth Continent, An Absolute Turkey (E15); e Centre (Islington Community Theatre); e Criminals, House of Bones, Medea, Colors rama Centre); Concrete Jungle (Riverside); e Riot Act, Beautiful Blows (The Mayhem mpany).

vision includes: **Live performance with Right d Fred (Celebrity Big Brother).**

briella Slade (Designer)

set and costume designer, theatre includes: **Murder Two (Watermill/The Other Palace); Romeo & let, Caucasian Chalk Circle, How Do You Eat Elephant? (National Youth Theatre Wales);** g of the Dump (Arts Theatre/UK tour); e Wind in the Willows, Alice In Wonderland tford Playhouse); Bumblescratch (West End); ry VI, Richard III (Wales Millennium Centre); use of Blakewell – We Can Make You Happy, e Birds, Happy Never After (Edinburgh ernational Festival); House of Blakewell's use Party (Latitude/Bestival/VAULT Festival); ad Born Grow (Frantic Assembly/National th Theatre Wales); She Loves Me, The House Bernarda Alba (GSA); The Blood is Strong borough); People Like Us (Pleasance).

ostume designer, theatre includes: **Working uthwark); In the Heights (Kings Cross/ thwark); Peter & the Starcatcher (Royal erngate, Northampton); Showstopper!** st End); The Last Five Years (St. James); Last Mermaid (Wales Millennium Centre); A istmas Carol, The Adventures of Pinocchio, One Hundred & One Dalmatians (Castle, llingborough); Just So, The Wind in the ows (South Hill Park); Everyday Maps for ryday Use (Finborough); Steve & Then It led (503).

ostume designer, dance includes: **The Green House, k (National Dance Company Wales).**

et and costume designer, opera includes: nmilitonen! (Welsh National Opera); The Iris rder (Traverse/UK tour); Albert Herring, si Fan Tutti (Dora Stouzker Hall).

Manjinder Virk (Dr Sharma)

For the Royal Court: **Free Outgoing, Workers Writes.**

Other theatre includes: **Redcrosse (RSC/Coventry Cathedral); Shabnam (& Naach), Unsuitable Girls (& Pilot); Autobiography of a Face (Lyric, Hammersmith); Bill Shakespeare's Italian Job (Gilded Balloon); Come Out Eli! (Recorded Delivery); Going Public (Tricycle/Red Room); Wintersun (Haymarket, Leicester); A Midsummer Night's Dream (Belgrade); Sleeping Beauty (London Bubble); The Millennium Mysteries (Belgrade/Teatro Biuro); The Magic Storybook (Unicorn).**

Television includes: **Bad Move, Midsomer Murders, Ordinary Lies, Brilliantman!, Call the Midwife, The Thick of It, Hunted, Monroe, Skins, Runaway, Britz, Plus One, Bradford Riots, Ghost Squad, Child of Mine, Green Wing, Ready When You Are Mr McGill, The Bill, Swiss Toni, Doctors, Trial by Jury.**

Film credits include: **With Love from Calais, Failure to Thrive, Kaleidoscope, The Sense of an Ending, History's Future, Out of Darkness, Broken Eternity, The Arbor, Lost Paradise, The Blue Tower World of Wrestling, Orange People, Two Minutes, Cross My Heart.**

THE ROYAL COURT THEATRE

The Royal Court Theatre is the writers' theatre. It is a leading force in world theatre for energetically cultivating writers – undiscovered, emerging and established.

Through the writers, the Royal Court is at the forefront of creating restless, alert, provocative theatre about now. We open our doors to the unheard voices and free thinkers that, through their writing, change our way of seeing.

Over 120,000 people visit the Royal Court in Sloane Square, London, each year and many thousands more see our work elsewhere through transfers to the West End and New York, UK and international tours, digital platforms, our residencies across London, and our site-specific work. Through all our work we strive to inspire audiences and influence future writers with radical thinking and provocative discussion.

The Royal Court's extensive development activity encompasses a diverse range of writers and artists and includes an ongoing programme of writers' attachments, readings, workshops and playwriting groups. Twenty years of the International Department's pioneering work around the world means the Royal Court has relationships with writers on every continent.

Within the past sixty years, John Osborne, Samuel Beckett, Arnold Wesker, Ann Jellicoe, Howard Brenton and David Hare have started their careers at the Court. Many others including Caryl Churchill, Athol Fugard, Mark Ravenhill, Simon Stephens, debbie tucker green, Sarah Kane - and, more recently, Lucy Kirkwood, Nick Payne, Penelope Skinner and Alistair McDowall - have followed.

The Royal Court has produced many iconic plays from Laura Wade's **Posh** to Jez Butterworth's **Jerusalem** and Martin McDonagh's **Hangmen**.

Royal Court plays from every decade are now performed on stage and taught in classrooms and universities across the globe.

It is because of this commitment to the writer that we believe there is no more important theatre in the world than the Royal Court.

Supported using public funding by
**ARTS COUNCIL
ENGLAND**

ROYAL

COMING UP IN 2017

20 Jun–7 Oct
Royal Court Theatre Productions,
Sonia Friedman Productions and
Neal Street Productions

The Ferryman
By Jez Butterworth
Directed by Sam Mendes

West End transfer
Gielgud Theatre

21 Jul–9 Sep
Road
By Jim Cartwright
Directed by John Tiffany

International Playwrights:
A Genesis Foundation Project
28 Sep–21 Oct
B
By Guillermo Calderón
Translated by William Gregory
Directed by Sam Pritchard

5 Oct–21 Oct
Victory Condition
By Chris Thorpe
Directed by Vicky Featherstone

Tickets from £12
royalcourttheatre.com

COURT

ROYAL COURT SUPPORTERS

The Royal Court is a registered charity and not-for-profit company. We need to raise £1.7 million every year in addition to our core grant from the Arts Council and our ticket income to achieve what we do.

We have significant and longstanding relationships with many generous organisations and individuals who provide vital support. Royal Court supporters enable us to remain the writers' theatre, find stories from everywhere and create theatre for everyone.

We can't do it without you.

PUBLIC FUNDING

Arts Council England, London
British Council

TRUSTS & FOUNDATIONS

The Bryan Adams Charitable Trust
The Austin & Hope Pilkington Trust
Martin Bowley Charitable Trust
Gerald Chapman Fund
CHK Charities
The City Bridge Trust
The Clifford Chance Foundation
Cockayne - Grants for the Arts
The Ernest Cook Trust
Cowley Charitable Trust
The Eranda Rothschild Foundation
Lady Antonia Fraser for The Pinter Commission
Genesis Foundation
The Golden Bottle Trust
The Haberdashers' Company
The Paul Hamlyn Foundation
Roderick & Elizabeth Jack
Jerwood Charitable Foundation
Kirsh Foundation
The Mackintosh Foundation
Marina Kleinwort Trust
The Andrew Lloyd Webber Foundation
The London Community Foundation
John Lyon's Charity

Clare McIntyre's Bursary
The Andrew W. Mellon Foundation
The Mercers' Company
The Portrack Charitable Trust
The David & Elaine Potter Foundation
The Richard Radcliffe Charitable Trust
Rose Foundation
Royal Victoria Hall Foundation
The Sackler Trust
The Sobell Foundation
John Thaw Foundation
The Garfield Weston Foundation

CORPORATE SPONSORS

Aqua Financial Solutions Ltd
Bloomberg
Cadogan Estates
Colbert
Edwardian Hotels, London
Fever-Tree
Gedye & Sons
Kirkland & Ellis International LLP
Kudos
MAC
Room One
Sister Pictures
Sky Drama

BUSINESS MEMBERS

Auerbach & Steele Opticians
CNC – Communications & Network Consulting
Cream
Lansons
Left Bank Pictures
Rockspring Property Investment Managers
Tetragon Financial Group
Vanity Fair

For more information or to become a foundation or business supporter contact Camilla Start: camillastart@ royalcourttheatre. com/020 7565 5064.

"There are no spaces, no rooms in my opinion, with a greater legacy of fearlessness, truth and clarity than this space."
Simon Stephens, Playwright in Residence

The Royal Court invests in the future of the theatre, offering writers the support, time and resources to find their voices and tell their stories, asking the big questions and responding to the issues of the moment.

As a registered charity, the Royal Court relies on the generous support of individuals to seek out, develop and nurture new voices. Please join us in Writing The Future by donating today.

You can donate online at royalcourttheatre.com/donate or via our donation box in the Bar & Kitchen.

We can't do it without you.

To find out more about the different ways in which you can be involved please contact Charlotte Cole on 020 7565 5049 / charlottecole@royalcourttheatre.com

BODIES

Vivienne Franzmann

Characters

CLEM, *forty-three*
JOSH, *early forties*
ONI, *late thirties*
DAVID, *seventies, has motor neurone disease*
DAUGHTER, *sixteen*
LAKSHMI, *early twenties*
DR SHARMA
BOY, *seven*
GIRL, *five*
CARER

The action takes place over nine months.

Note on Text

A dash on its own line indicates a beat.

Two dashes indicate a pause.

Three or more dashes lasts longer.

This text went to press before the end of rehearsals and so may differ slightly from the play as performed.

One

Clem's House

CLEM *and* DAUGHTER.

DAUGHTER. What are these?

CLEM. Crisps.

DAUGHTER. Crisps?

CLEM. Kale crisps.

DAUGHTER. Kale crisps?

CLEM. Yeah, crisps made out of kale.

DAUGHTER. Crisps made out of kale?

CLEM. Can you stop repeating everything I –

DAUGHTER. Can you stop repeating everything I –

CLEM. Very good. LOL.

DAUGHTER. Please don't say LOL.

CLEM (*offering*). Kale crisp?

DAUGHTER (*picks one up*). This is not a crisp. It's not crisp.
    This is a flake. It's a kale flake.

CLEM. Try it.

DAUGHTER. No thanks.

CLEM. Go on. YOLO.

DAUGHTER. Don't.

—

CLEM. I made them.

DAUGHTER. You made these?

CLEM. Yeah, you get a bag of kale, get rid of the stalky parts, separate all the bits, cover them in oil, mustard, honey, lemon juice and tarragon and bake them for fifteen minutes. You turn the oven off and let them rest for fifteen minutes.

DAUGHTER. Jesus.

CLEM. They're delicious. They are absolutely –

DAUGHTER. Have we got any proper crisps?

CLEM. No.

DAUGHTER. Fuck.

CLEM. Don't say fuck. And you told me not to buy any proper crisps.

DAUGHTER. I didn't tell you to –

CLEM. You said you didn't want me to get any crisps, because of the trans-fats thing. You said you thought the trans fats were giving you cancer and making you fat.

DAUGHTER. Yeah, but I didn't mean it. Obviously, I didn't mean it.

—

CLEM. Top cupboard.

DAUGHTER *gets out a packet of Kettle Chips.*

DAUGHTER. The thing is, I did mean it. When I said that about the trans fats and the cancer and getting fat, I completely meant it.

CLEM. I know.

DAUGHTER. No, you didn't. You wouldn't have bought –

CLEM. I know you. I know you from the tips of your fingers to the ends of your hair to your weird little toe that points outwards like Daddy's.

DAUGHTER. Do you mean my 'special toe'?

CLEM. When you were little, we –

DAUGHTER. Yeah, alright.

CLEM. It was so sweet, the way –

DAUGHTER. Yep.

CLEM. It was –

DAUGHTER. Okay.

CLEM. So perfect.

—

DAUGHTER. You should have got the small bags.

—

I'm going to have to eat the whole thing now.

CLEM. Or you could eat half and put the rest back in the cupboard for later.

DAUGHTER. I could if I was a totally different person. If I was you.

—

—

Aren't you going to stop me?

CLEM. No.

DAUGHTER. Even though you know these are really bad for me and I've got no self-control.

CLEM. What you do with your body is your business.

DAUGHTER. You don't say that about smoking.

CLEM. Smoking kills.

DAUGHTER. Trans fats kill. Do you want some?

CLEM. No thanks, I've got these delicious oil-and-mustard-and-honey-and-lemon-juice-and-tarragon-infused kale crisps.

—

DAUGHTER. Weird word. Tarragon.

CLEM. It's a herb. It's like –

DAUGHTER. I know what it is.

—

It tastes like aniseed and grows wild in Europe and North America.

—

What?

CLEM. How do you know that?

DAUGHTER. How does anyone know anything?

CLEM. Someone tells you. You learn it at school. You read it in a book. You go on the internet. You look for it.

DAUGHTER. Some things you just know. You don't know how, you just do.

—

Stop looking at me like that.

CLEM. Like what?

DAUGHTER. Like that.

CLEM. I'm proud of you.

DAUGHTER. Because I know about tarragon?

CLEM. Because of the person that you are.

—

—

It seems like yesterday we were holding you in our arms and wondering what you were going to be like. You were so tiny, so gorgeous – a tiny gorgeous little bird who we had waited –

DAUGHTER. What's your favourite bird?

—

CLEM. A finch.

DAUGHTER. Like Granddad.

—

CLEM. When I was little and he used to breed them, I'd feed the ones that had been rejected by their mothers with –

DAUGHTER. Why do animals do that? I mean, they go to all the trouble of conceiving, and from what I've heard of the foxes fucking in the middle of the night that doesn't sound like it's up to much, and then they give birth or sit on a nest for a million years until it hatches and then they just say, sod it, I'm not into this any more, you're on your own.

CLEM. Something instinctive, I guess.

DAUGHTER. Surely the instinct should be to look after them, continue the genes, protect their bloodline, whatever. That's instinct.

—

—

I like crows. Crows are cool.

—

There's something about crows, isn't there?

—

They're sleek and their eyes shine and their feathers are beautiful like oil.

CLEM. A crow got into my dad's aviary once. Destroyed everything. It was awful.

DAUGHTER. How did it get in there?

CLEM. Don't know.

DAUGHTER. Probably opened the latch with its beak.

CLEM. I doubt it, it's only a –

DAUGHTER. Crows are so clever. At my school, there's this one that waits until break's over and then goes through the bins, picks out the crisp packets with its beak, eats all the bits and then chucks each bag on the floor. One Year 7 class got a detention for littering their playground and it was the crow all along.

—

—

I think I might be a crow.

—

I said I think I might be a –

CLEM. I heard you.

—

I'm just trying to figure out what that actually means.

DAUGHTER. It means I'm a crow.

—

CLEM. You're not going to get a tattoo, are you? That's not what this is leading to, is it? Wings on your back. Not a horrible black feather along your arm or anything like that. Please don't do that. Promise me you won't do that.

—

Promise me you won't do anything to your skin.

DAUGHTER. It's my body.

CLEM. Your skin has always been so beautiful, why would you want to mutilate your –

DAUGHTER. I'm not getting a tattoo.

CLEM. Promise.

—

Promise.

DAUGHTER. I promise.

—

—

—

CLEM. Which school do you go to?

DAUGHTER. Creighton.

—

It's on Wellington Lane.

CLEM. Where the lido is?

DAUGHTER. Was. They demolished it to build the school.

CLEM. When?

DAUGHTER. About nine years ago.

—

—

CLEM. It's not private, is it?

DAUGHTER. No.

CLEM. Good. I thought not. I would never… It's not something that I think is… Not that your father agrees with me. I keep telling him, my dad will kill me if we…well, it's not just that. I don't believe in it.

—

Is it a good school?

DAUGHTER. Rated outstanding three times. Says so on a banner outside the gates. Lacking a bit of humility that.

CLEM. And you're a good student?

DAUGHTER. Six A-stars, three As and a B.

CLEM. And you like it there?

DAUGHTER. Yeah.

CLEM. You're happy?

DAUGHTER. Yeah.

CLEM. Yeah?

DAUGHTER. Yes. I'm happy.

—

—

CLEM. Are you going to go to university?

DAUGHTER. That's ages away.

CLEM. It'll be here in a moment. Before we can even blink. That's what they say. Time twists. It twists and it turns. One moment you're holding your… You're holding your…

DAUGHTER. Are you alright?

—

CLEM. And the next she's off doing her own thing, with her own life, making her own choices and mistakes, and you've spent all that time wishing and wondering and hoping that she'll be all you've ever wanted her to be and you cross your fingers that you've done a good job as you send her out into the world.

—

—

—

Are you a crow?

DAUGHTER. No.

CLEM. Are you here?

—

Are you –

DAUGHTER. Yes.

CLEM. Because for a moment, I thought maybe…

DAUGHTER. I'm here.

—

CLEM. Because I don't think I can…

—

I couldn't bear it if…

DAUGHTER. I'm here.

—

CLEM. You're all I've ever wanted.

DAUGHTER. I know.

CLEM. I don't think you do.

DAUGHTER. I do.

CLEM. How can you possibly…

DAUGHTER. Everything will be okay now.

—

I'll warm your heart.

—

I'll hold it in my hands like a baby finch.

—

I'll make the pain go that squeezes your windpipe and fills your lungs.

—

I'll make you feel clean and light again. Propel you into the air like a sycamore seed.

—

I'll make up for all the others.

—

I promise, Mummy.

—

Breathe.

—

Mummy, remember to breathe.

Two

India

Waiting room. A small room. Fertility clinic. JOSH sits. CLEM enters. She sits down, pulls out a book. It's a Hindi phrase book.

—

JOSH. Have you been smoking?

—

Have you?

—

I can't believe you've been smoking.

—

Give me one.

CLEM. No.

JOSH. I haven't had a fag in –

CLEM. Nor me.

JOSH. You just had one.

—

What was it like?

CLEM. Awful. Gum?

—

—

JOSH. What brand did you get?

CLEM. Marlboro Lights.

JOSH. Why did you get Marlboro Lights?

CLEM. Healthier.

JOSH. God, I remember Marlboro Lights.

CLEM. And they're just how you remember them. Gross.

—

JOSH. I'm surprised they sell Marlboro Lights here.

CLEM. They sell Marlboro Lights everywhere.

—

JOSH. Please.

CLEM. No.

JOSH. Give me one.

CLEM. Can't.

JOSH. Don't be such a –

CLEM. I only bought one.

—

There's a man on a stand. He's got a lighter on a string
attached to his stall. It's a good system. Reminds me of school.

JOSH. Not my school.

CLEM. The newsagent used to sell single fags to us on the way
home. It was brilliant.

JOSH. Sounds it.

CLEM. Yep, a fag and a can of 7Up on the back of the 125 bus.

JOSH. Such a chav.

CLEM. Don't say chav.

JOSH. It's –

CLEM. Don't say it.

JOSH. It's –

CLEM. Offensive.

JOSH. Yeah, but –

CLEM. Would you say chav in front of my dad?

JOSH. Probably… not.

CLEM. Why not?

JOSH. Because he'd give me the socialist stare, call up his union mates and my bollocks would shrivel to acorns.

CLEM. Shrivel to?

JOSH. You know I've got the bollocks of a baboon.

—

Yeah?

—

Say it.

CLEM. Shut up.

JOSH. Go on. Say it.

CLEM. I'm not going to –

JOSH. Say it.

CLEM. I've got the bollocks of a baboon.

JOSH. I knew you were going to do that. You always do that. You're hugely predictable and massively boring. I don't know why I put up with you.

—

—

—

How was your dad?

CLEM. Fine.

—

JOSH. What did he say?

CLEM. Wished us luck.

—

What?

JOSH. Nothing.

CLEM. Please don't.

JOSH. I didn't say anything.

CLEM. Stop it.

JOSH. What?

CLEM. Thinking it.

JOSH. What? I'm not –

CLEM. Thinking about him. I don't want you thinking about him.

JOSH. Christ, the actual thought police, the literal actual total –

CLEM. If you're thinking about him then I'm thinking about him.

JOSH. You're the one who brought him up in the –

CLEM. I don't want to think about him. Just for a moment.
Not now.

—

—

—

JOSH. Maybe I'll go and –

CLEM. Sit down.

—

Sit. (*Looks in book, Hindi.*) *Baithiye!*

—

—

—

—

JOSH. I'm sweating like a pig in the desert.

—

Like a pig in a sauna.

—

Like a pig in a spit.

—

On a spit. Like a pig on a spit. I need some fresh air.

CLEM. You won't find any out there.

JOSH. But –

CLEM. It's a thousand degrees. And polluted to fuck.

—

JOSH. Maybe, I'll just –

CLEM. I know what you're doing.

JOSH. This place is –

CLEM. I know exactly what you're doing.

—

One puff kills a million sperm.

JOSH. You made that up.

CLEM. Nope.

JOSH. Convenient it's exactly a million.

CLEM. My eggs are rotten. Your sperm is fine. Let's keep it
that way.

—

—

—

JOSH. Are you going to come in with me?

—

While I do it.

—

You could help.

CLEM. What, like many hands make light work?

JOSH. Just thought you might like to be involved.

—

It's a momentous occasion. You might regret it otherwise.

—

Do you think they'll ask if you want to come in with me?

CLEM. This is a serious medical establishment. They're not
going to expect us to toddle off for a romantic wank in one
of their sterile booths.

—

—

—

—

—

We should have brought a gift.

—

Something for her kids. Something from home.

—

Like a money box that looks like double-decker bus or
Union Jack T-shirts or maybe –

JOSH. We've brought a gift. It's called twenty-two thousand
pounds.

—

LAKSHMI *opens the door. She walks past them. They watch
her. She knocks on an inner door.* DR SHARMA *appears at
the window.* LAKSHMI *is waved away and told to enter
a different way. She turns round and goes out. She walks
round the back and disappears through a different door.*

—

—

—

I can't believe you smoked.

—

Without me.

—

The first fag in nine years and you did it without me.

CLEM. You can smoke afterwards.

JOSH. Yeah?

CLEM. Why not?

JOSH. Yeah.

CLEM. We'll get a pack of twenty and smoke the whole
bloody lot.

—

JOSH. Clementine Kennedy-Clarke, I fucking love you.

—

Three

David's House

Living room. CLEM, DAVID *and* ONI. DAVID *in a chair.*

CLEM. What happened to Sandra?

ONI. The agency rang me and told me to come and –

CLEM. Yes, but what happened to Sandra?

ONI. She's not working –

CLEM. Dad, do you know what happened to –

DAVID. Not here.

CLEM. I know she's not here.

DAVID. Oni.

CLEM. What?

DAVID. Oni.

ONI. My name's Oni.

CLEM. I don't mean to be rude, but I don't understand why –

DAVID. Clementine…

CLEM. My father has complex needs and –

DAVID. She knows.

ONI. I have the notes.

–

CLEM. When did you – ?

ONI. Three days ago.

CLEM. Three days ago?

ONI. Yes.

CLEM. The evenings as well?

ONI. No, Meera has been in.

—

You don't have to worry. I am a nice person.

DAVID. Very nice person.

CLEM. What?

DAVID. Very nice person.

CLEM. I'm not suggesting she's – I'm not suggesting you're not a nice person.

—

What did the agency say?

ONI. They asked me to come here and –

CLEM. Did the physio come yesterday?

ONI. Yes.

CLEM. And the nurse?

ONI. Audrey?

CLEM. Yes.

ONI. She came the day before. And the speech therapist this morning.

—

CLEM. Okay.

—

ONI. Everything is under control.

DAVID. Yes. Under control.

—

CLEM. But the agency should have told me –

DAVID. You weren't here.

—

ONI. Clementine, would you like a cup of tea?

CLEM. No, thank you.

ONI. I have Boasters. Do you want –

CLEM. No.

—

Thank you.

—

—

ONI. David, your – (*Adjusts cushion*.)

—

That's better.

—

You ready for some lunch?

DAVID. Please.

ONI (*to* CLEM). Do you want something to eat?

CLEM. No.

ONI. I can make you a sandwich.

CLEM. It's okay.

ONI. A cheese sandwich for you.

CLEM. No, I –

ONI. Pickle. Mayonnaise.

CLEM. No, really, it's –

ONI. Cathedral Extra Mature. I can –

CLEM. No.

—

Thank you. No.

—

ONI *goes*.

—

How are you feeling?

—

How's everything going?

—

With…

DAVID. Oni.

CLEM. Oni.

DAVID. Good.

CLEM. Good.

—

—

—

DAVID. Not her fault Sandra's gone.

—

CLEM. Sorry, Dad, say it again, I didn't –

DAVID. Sandra. Not her fault.

CLEM. Yes, well, the agency should have –

DAVID. Apologise to her.

CLEM. What?

DAVID. Should apologise.

CLEM. I don't need to apo–

DAVID. Rude.

—

Rude.

—

—

CLEM. Did Sandra say she was leaving?

DAVID. No.

CLEM. She must have said something.

DAVID. No.

CLEM. But –

DAVID. Just a job.

—

A job.

CLEM. But she seemed very fond of you and –

DAVID. Maybe she got more money.

—

Another job.

CLEM. Maybe she went back to Kenya.

DAVID. Uganda.

CLEM. I thought she was from –

DAVID. No.

CLEM. But she talked about Nairobi.

DAVID. Uganda.

CLEM. Right. Okay. I don't know why I thought that.

—

Shall we go outside?

—

Do you want to go outside to the aviary?

DAVID. It's lunch.

CLEM. Just for a moment.

—

How are the birds?

—

We can come back in a minute. Come on, let's…

DAVID. I have to eat.

CLEM. But –

DAVID. No.

—

—

—

ONI *comes in*.

ONI. You want some mashed apple with the banana?

DAVID. Please.

—

CLEM. Oni?

—

About earlier, I didn't meant to be…

ONI. No problem.

CLEM. It's just, Sandra's been with Dad for quite a few months and I was surprised that she'd –

ONI. I understand.

CLEM. I was worried, that's all.

ONI. Darling, there's no problem.

She goes.

—

—

—

CLEM. I heard you got a job as a dentist, how is it?

—

I heard you got a job as a dentist, how is it?

—

I heard you got a job as a dentist –

DAVID. Just filling in.

—

Just filling in.

CLEM. Ha, yeah, but do you know the drill?

—

DAVID. I heard you got a job as a ferry driver…

—

CLEM. A what?

DAVID. Ferry driver.

—

CLEM. I heard you got a job as a ferry driver… Yeah, right. Shit. Wait. Wait.

—

—

—

The interview was plain sailing.

DAVID. Too slow.

CLEM. Since when was there a time limit?

DAVID. Too slow.

—

   Speed.

CLEM. Yeah, but there's never been a time limit.

DAVID. Got to be fast.

CLEM. Okay, hit me. Go again.

   ONI *comes in, gives* CLEM *a cup of tea, sets one down next to* DAVID.

DAVID. Heard you got job as professor.

—

   Professor.

ONI. I thought you were a television producer.

CLEM. It's a game. We're playing a –

ONI. I saw *The Fattest Man in the World*.

CLEM. That wasn't mine. That was Channel 5.

ONI. I thought you made that.

CLEM. No, I made *The World's Fattest Man*. It was on Channel 4. It was –

ONI. Yes, that's the one I saw.

CLEM. Oh, right. Okay. So… Okay.

ONI. It was very sad. Did you see it, David?

DAVID. No.

CLEM. Dad's seen my other stuff though, like the show I made about FGM, which you thought was good, didn't you?

DAVID. Very good.

CLEM. And the series about the adolescent mental-health unit up in Scotland. That was –

ONI. What I didn't understand was why did Jeff's wife keep feeding him?

—

They had to knock a hole in the wall of his house to get him out.

—

It was awful.

She goes.

CLEM. I've got something for you.

She gets a parcel out of her bag. She goes to give it to him. He takes it. He starts opening it.

Do you need me to… (*Gestures at parcel.*)

DAVID. Can do it.

It's a struggle to open it.

Get my glasses.

CLEM *gets his glasses from the side. He looks at the present. It's an Indian cotton shirt.*

—

—

Thank you.

CLEM. My pleasure.

—

Do you want to put it – (*Gestures him wearing it.*)

DAVID. No.

CLEM. Okay.

—

—

—

Do you want to ask me anything about –

DAVID. No.

—

ONI *comes in with a tray.*

ONI. Right. Nearly there. (*Sees the shirt.*) Oh my word, what
  is –

CLEM. I bought it for Dad. It's from India.

ONI (*picks it up, holds it against him*). You look like Salman
  Khan.

—

Bollywood actor. Killed a homeless man. Got away with it.
(*Looks at it.*) It's very beautiful. (*Folds it up.*) Let's save it
for special occasions. Like the arrival of your grandchild.

She organises DAVID, *straightening him up. Puts a sheet of
kitchen towel on the front of his T-shirt.*

What do you think, Clem?

ONI *pulls the table across. Puts the spoon in his hand. He
slowly begins to eat.*

For the impending grandchild.

—

Sorry. Am I not…

—

I thought…

DAVID. I told her.

ONI. I'll be quiet. It's –

CLEM. No, it's fine –

ONI. Are you sure? I –

CLEM. Really, it's –

ONI. I didn't know it was a secret.

CLEM. It's not a secret.

ONI. Because if it is, I'll just –

CLEM. It's not.

ONI. Phew. Good. Nearly got you in some hot shit there, David.

–

–

My sister's friend was a surrogate. It's an amazing thing to do for another woman.

CLEM. Yes, yes it is.

ONI. To give your eggs and your body to –

CLEM. We're not using her eggs.

DAVID. Russian.

CLEM. The egg donor is Russian.

ONI. In India?

CLEM. The agency found her. They've a sister clinic in Russia.

ONI. But the surrogate is Indian?

CLEM. Yes, the surrogate is Indian.

–

ONI. Oh, I see…

CLEM. –

ONI. Of course, so the baby's skin will be –

CLEM. No, that's not…

ONI. But you want the baby to –

CLEM. We thought…

ONI. And with the Russian donor, the baby will be –

CLEM. We just thought –

ONI. You want her to look like you.

—

CLEM. Yes.

ONI. Like you and your husband.

CLEM. Yes, as much as is possible, like me and Josh.

ONI. Of course, why wouldn't you?

—

CLEM. It's not that we want to hide anything. It's just, you know…

ONI. Easier.

CLEM. Yes. No. It means less questions about… Do you think we'll have a girl?

—

You said –

ONI. Do you want a girl?

CLEM. I don't mind.

DAVID. You can choose.

—

Can choose.

CLEM. We're not doing that.

DAVID. You always wanted a girl.

CLEM. We're just going to wait and see if any of the embryos implant and whichever ones, if any –

DAVID. Rather fatalistic given circumstances.

–

Fatalistic given –

ONI. He said rather fatalistic given that you can –

CLEM. Thanks. I know what he said.

–

–

–

ONI. So amazing you can do this, isn't it, David?

–

–

Science is incredible.

CLEM. Yep.

ONI. My husband is a scientist.

CLEM. Is he?

ONI. A haematologist. He works at a university back at home. He's with my daughter.

ONI *gets a photo out of her purse and shows* CLEM.

She's twelve. Running him ragged. I tell him it will only get worse when she hits the teens, so he better pray that he's over here by then and I can take control of the situation.

She points to the photo.

My son. AJ. He's sixteen. He's here with me.

–

DAVID. He got As in all exams.

ONI. Yes, but still can't tidy his bedroom, little bastard.

DAVID. All As.

ONI. David thinks I'm too hard on him. Did you meet the donor?

CLEM. What?

ONI. The Russian donor, did you –

CLEM. No.

ONI. The surrogate?

CLEM. No. But we know all about her. She's got two children of
her own. A boy and a girl. She wants to send them to school.
And the money will mean she can do that and have enough for
a business or a house or whatever she wants to do.

—

And she stays at the clinic for the nine months, so she'll be
cared for properly. Not at the clinic, but a place the clinic has
for the women. A centre.

ONI. And her children as well?

CLEM. No, they're with her husband. Their father. Back home
in their village.

—

—

DAVID. What's her name?

—

Her name.

CLEM. Lakshmi.

—

—

ONI. And when will you know?

CLEM. Any day now.

ONI. Amazing.

—

Well, fingers crossed.

CLEM. Thanks. Yeah. Fingers crossed.

—

CLEM *looks at* DAVID. *He looks at her. He looks away.*

—

Four

Clem's House

CLEM *hands* JOSH *a parcel. He looks at it.*

—

He opens the parcel. Inside is another parcel wrapped in tissue paper. He opens it. Inside is a babygro. He holds it up, looks at her.

CLEM. Couldn't help it. I'm a naff bastard.

Different ages of the same DAUGHTER *run in – playing and giggling, jumping on the table, crawling under the chairs, filling the room with noise and laughter. The last* DAUGHTER *in the space is the oldest one, sixteen years.* CLEM *looks at her. They smile at each other.*

—

JOSH *goes to* CLEM. *He kisses her.*

—

Five

Clem's House

CLEM *and* DAUGHTER.

DAUGHTER. The third time was terrible, wasn't it?

—

The one in the middle.

—

You thought that one was going to stick, didn't you?

—

You could feel it. You could feel it wedge in.

CLEM. I was ready.

—

I was completely ready. I felt… I felt like a…

DAUGHTER. Like a superwoman.

CLEM. Yes, like a superwoman.

DAUGHTER. You were strong enough to pick up a house.

CLEM. Yes.

DAUGHTER. You could pull down the sky.

—

What happened?

CLEM. Nothing. Nothing happened.

DAUGHTER. But you thought it was going to –

CLEM. I'm a fool.

DAUGHTER. You're too hard on yourself.

—

Not everyone can be a mother.

CLEM. Don't say that.

DAUGHTER. That's what your mum said.

—

And then she said, think of all the things you'll be able to do without children. And you pushed her.

CLEM. I didn't mean to.

DAUGHTER. You started to cry and you pushed her.

CLEM. Yes, but I didn't mean –

DAUGHTER. You did. You were furious.

CLEM. No, I –

DAUGHTER. You were –

CLEM. But –

DAUGHTER. She hit her head on the corner cabinet and the blood started gushing out.

CLEM. Please, don't. That was –

DAUGHTER. She had to get a stitch from A&E.

CLEM. I know, but I was –

DAUGHTER. You ignored her phone calls for three weeks after.

CLEM. Why are you –

DAUGHTER. So you remember.

CLEM. I don't want to remember.

DAUGHTER. You have to.

CLEM. I don't want –

DAUGHTER. So you don't lose sight.

CLEM. I don't know why you're –

DAUGHTER. You have to remember what you've been through.

—

All of it.

—

—

Your mum was already dead by the fifth one, wasn't she?

—

The near-miss.

—

The one that nearly made it.

—

The one with little hands and feet and eyes.

—

The one that was going to be a doctor or beauty therapist or a judo instructor.

—

The one that the teachers were going to say was funny.

—

She's such a quiet gregarious studious reckless ray of sunshine and bother. She's quite a piece of work. Your daughter is quite something.

—

You would have killed a city full of people to protect her.

CLEM. Yes.

DAUGHTER. Is that what the surrogate is feeling?

—

Do you think the surrogate has a heart bursting with love for me?

—

Full of possibilities.

—

Guarding me with her life.

—

Roaring like a lion.

CLEM. No.

—

You're not her baby.

DAUGHTER. No, I'm not.

CLEM. You're mine.

DAUGHTER. Yes. Sorry. I'm yours.

—

—

Six

Clem's House/Fertility Clinic Skype

CLEM, JOSH, DR SHARMA *and* LAKSHMI *on Skype*.

LAKSHMI *is visible to* CLEM *and* JOSH. CLEM *and* JOSH *are not visible to her.* DAUGHTER *watches*.

—

DR SHARMA (*Hindi*). *Voh tumhe achi tarah dekhna chahtey hain. Line pay aa jao.* [They want you to see you properly. Move to the line, please.]

LAKSHMI *moves forward*.

DR SHARMA (*Hindi*). *Line pay khadhe ho jao.* [Stand on the line.]

CLEM. Lakshmi, can you move forward a little bit please?

DR SHARMA (*Hindi*). *Thodha aage ho jao. Aapne payr line par rakho.* [Put your toes on the line.]

LAKSHMI *puts her toes on the line*.

CLEM. Thank you, Lakshmi.

DR SHARMA (*to* CLEM). Is she clearly visible to you?

CLEM. Yes, that's fine.

DR SHARMA (*to* LAKSHMI, *Hindi*). *Is taraf mudh jao.* [Turn to the side.]

LAKSHMI *turns to the side*.

JOSH. I can't really see anything there. (*To* CLEM.) Can you?

DR SHARMA. She is just twelve weeks, remember.

CLEM. Of course. She'll barely show, so it's not really –

JOSH. She's a lime.

—

The baby's a lime.

—

The baby's the size of a lime. Or is it a fig? Hold on, hold on, I think I can see something. Yes. No. Actually, no.

DR SHARMA (*Hindi*). *Aapney kapdhe utaro*. [Remove your clothing.]

LAKSHMI *removes her sari*.

Lakshmi is in excellent health and everything is progressing as we would expect.

CLEM (*to* JOSH, *motions to go*). Oh, maybe you should –

JOSH. Dr Sharma, should I…

DR SHARMA. She has been sleeping very well and –

JOSH. I can go out for this bit, while you –

DR SHARMA. It is fine.

CLEM (*to* JOSH). I think you should –

JOSH. But I want to see –

CLEM. Come back in when she's –

DR SHARMA. Really, it is fine.

LAKSHMI *stands in her underwear.* CLEM *and* JOSH *scrutinise.*

(*Hindi.*) *Sidha khadhe ho jao.* [Stand up straight.]

—

(*Hindi.*) *Aapney hath nichey rakho. Unko dekhney do.* [Put your hands down. Let them see.]

LAKSHMI *puts her hands down to her sides*.

JOSH. Fuck. Look at that. Sorry. Yeah. Fuck. Sorry. Fuck. That's our baby. Is that our –

DR SHARMA. Yes, Mr Kennedy-Clarke.

JOSH. Clem? You can see, right?

CLEM. Yes.

—

JOSH. It's happening. It's actually fucking happening. Sorry about the swearing, doctor, it's just –

DR SHARMA. You're excited.

JOSH. Can you tell her to push it out.

–

Push her belly out.

CLEM (*to* JOSH). Don't be so –

DR SHARMA. Yes, I can ask her.

CLEM. Don't ask her to do that. (*To* JOSH.) That's so –

JOSH. Okay, don't ask her. Veto that.

DR SHARMA. I can ask her –

JOSH. Sorry. No, don't. That was stupid of me.

–

DR SHARMA. We are very pleased with the baby's progress. And Lakshmi is excellent.

–

She's made friends with the other ladies in the centre. It's a very supportive environment. They take –

JOSH. Can you ask her to turn to the left a little bit.

DR SHARMA (*Hindi*). *Bayen hath ki taraf mudho*. [Turn to the left.]

LAKSHMI *turns to the left*.

JOSH. God, you can really… Clem, look…

–

DR SHARMA. Is there anything else you'd like to ask her.

JOSH. Tell her that she's made us the happiest people ever. Tell her that.

DR SHARMA (*Hindi*). *Yeh kahtey hain ki tumney inko bahut khush kiya hai*. [He says you've made them very happy.]

LAKSHMI *smiles*.

She is pleased.

JOSH. Do we have the date for the caesarean?

DR SHARMA. We are not quite there yet, so –

JOSH. Obviously, we'd like to book the flights sooner rather than later.

DR SHARMA. Of course.

JOSH. So as soon as you know the date, you'll let me know.

DR SHARMA. Yes, of course.

CLEM *looks at* DAUGHTER.

CLEM. Can you ask her something for me?

DR SHARMA. Of course.

CLEM. Can you ask her how it feels?

DR SHARMA (*Hindi*). *Tumhara kaysa haal hai?* [How do you feel?]

LAKSHMI (*Hindi*). *Main Khush hun*. [I am happy.]

DR SHARMA. She is happy.

DAUGHTER *motions for* CLEM *to ask again*.

CLEM. I mean, how does it feel having our baby growing inside her?

DR SHARMA. It is tiring for her, but she's –

CLEM. No, I mean, how does she feel with our baby growing inside her rather than her own, what is that like for her?

DR SHARMA. She is looking forward very much to giving you your child.

CLEM. Can you ask her how she feels about having our child inside her?

JOSH. Why are you –

CLEM. Ask her, please.

DR SHARMA (*Hindi*). *Yeh puchti hai ki tumhain kaysa lagta hai ki inka bacha tumharey ander badh raha hai.* [She wants to know what it is like having their baby grow inside of you?]

LAKSHMI (*slowly, English*). Happy to make dreams come true.

—

JOSH. That's lovely. Thank you, Lakshmi.

DAUGHTER *leans against the wall and watches* CLEM. LAKSHMI *steps up close to the screen.*

DR SHARMA (*Hindi*). *Yeh na karo.* [Don't do that.]

JOSH. Hi. Hiya, Lakshmi.

DR SHARMA (*Hindi*). *Hat jao vahan say.* [Come away.]

LAKSHMI *looks back at the screen. She touches it.*

CLEM. What's she –

DR SHARMA. This kind of technology is unusual for her. (*Hindi.*) *Vapis idhar aao.* [Come away now.]

JOSH. Does she want to see us?

DR SHARMA. No, no. (*Hindi.*) *Pichey line pay aa jao.* [Go back to the line.]

JOSH. She can see us if she wants.

CLEM. Josh, I don't think –

DR SHARMA (*Hindi*). *Lakshmi, Line pay vapis aa jao.* [Lakshmi, return to the line.]

JOSH. It's only fair. We can see her, let's just –

CLEM. No.

He clicks the visibility icon. They appear on the screen.
LAKSHMI *stops. She stares at them. A moment.*

JOSH. *Namaste, Lakshmi.*

LAKSHMI *bursts out laughing.* JOSH *starts laughing.*

DR SHARMA. I must apologise for –

CLEM. It's okay.

DR SHARMA (*Hindi*). *Bas karo.* [Stop now.]

CLEM. Josh…

DR SHARMA (*Hindi*). *Manay kaha na Bas karo.* [I said stop.]

JOSH (*laughing*). This is so…

CLEM (*to* JOSH). Stop it. (*Starts laughing.*) Sorry, Dr Sharma.

DR SHARMA. No problem.

JOSH (*laughing*). This has to be the weirdest thing that anyone
has ever done. Seriously, this is –

CLEM (*laughing*). Stop it, you're making me… stop it.

LAKSHMI *looks at them.*

Lakshmi, we are so grateful to you. If you need anything,
anything at all, you just have to ask.

DR SHARMA (*Hindi*). *Yeh tera shukria karna chahtey hain.*
[She says they are very grateful to you.]

CLEM. Without you, we –

JOSH *still laughing.*

Shut up, Josh, seriously. (*To* LAKSHMI.) You've changed
our lives. Having a child is all we've ever wanted.

DR SHARMA (*Hindi*). *Yeh kahti hai ki tumnain inki zindagi
badal di hai. Inki siraf ek itcha thi ki bacha ho.* [She says
you've changed their lives. Having a child is all they've
wanted.]

LAKSHMI *turns away.*

CLEM. What is it?

DR SHARMA. She is emotional. It is to be expected. (*Hindi*.) *Mudh jao*. [Turn around.]

LAKSHMI *turns around to face them*.

—

DAUGHTER *looks at* CLEM.

—

Seven

David's House

CLEM, DAVID *and* ONI *gathered round an iPad*. DAVID *is wearing a neck brace*.

CLEM. So I've downloaded them for you. And all you have to do to access them is click here and then here and… And then…

An audiobook of Bleak House *plays. A few seconds*. CLEM *reaches over and turns it off*.

Now you do it.

—

—

What's the first thing you need to do?

ONI. Shall I write the instructions down?

CLEM. Yes, that would be helpful.

DAVID. Not idiot.

CLEM. No one's saying you're an idiot.

DAVID. Good.

ONI. You're a luddite.

DAVID. Bloody cheek.

—

CLEM. So what do you do now?

DAVID *presses the buttons*. Bleak House *starts playing*.

Bingo.

They listen to it again. DAVID *pauses it.*

CLEM. I wasn't sure what you'd like other than Dickens.
There's quite a lot of free ones on YouTube as well and
there's poetry and stuff. I'll show you that another time.

ONI. I can show him.

CLEM. And what's really good as well is that now we can
Skype. You've heard of Skype?

DAVID. Course.

ONI. He hasn't.

DAVID. I have.

ONI. You told me –

DAVID. I have.

ONI. Liar, you said –

CLEM. Anyway it's really easy. I've set it up, so we're all good
to go.

ONI. I can show him if you're in a hurry.

CLEM. I'm not in a hurry.

—

ONI. We Skype my husband and daughter. Sometimes it freezes
in very ugly positions. Me and my son laugh our asses off
about my husband's expressions when it sticks. He's a
handsome man, but by God, he pulls some faces.

—

This is a very good one. Very good quality.

—

My last client had one of these. He said it was very intuitive.

DAVID. What happened to him?

ONI. What?

DAVID. What happened him?

ONI. He died, David.

—

DAVID. Could have got his for free.

ONI *laughs*.

CLEM. What? What did you –

DAVID. We could have got his for free.

CLEM. Say it again, Dad, I didn't –

DAVID. For free.

—

ONI. He said we could have got his iPad for free.

—

Because he's dead. He doesn't need it any more.

—

It's a joke.

CLEM. Yes, I know it's a –

ONI. Your father is a comedian.

CLEM. Yes. Yes, he is.

—

ONI. Tell Clementine the joke.

—

Go on.

—

CLEM. What joke?

ONI. He's got a funny joke about Essex girls.

CLEM. Essex girls?

ONI. Yes, you know the girls that live in Essex. *TOWIE*. Chingford.

—

Tell Clementine the joke.

DAVID. Won't like it.

ONI. Of course she'll like it.

CLEM. I love a joke. I love jokes.

DAVID. Not this one.

ONI. Tell it. She'll like it.

CLEM. Go on, Dad.

DAVID. Terry told me.

CLEM. Terry?

DAVID. Terry from the union.

—

Big Terry.

CLEM. When was he –

ONI. He came last week. Popped in. Brought a pie. A... what was it?

DAVID. Ale pie. Fat bastard.

CLEM. Was it good to see him?

DAVID. Yeah. Like old days.

—

Old days.

—

ONI. David, tell Clementine your joke.

DAVID. Honestly, she won't –

ONI. Stop making excuses and tell the bloody joke.

DAVID. But she –

ONI. What do Essex girls use as protection in sex?

—

The bus shelter.

—

—

DAVID. Told you.

—

CLEM. What? I'm laughing.

—

ONI. You don't like it?

CLEM. I like it. It's fine. It's a bit…

ONI. It's funny because the Essex girls have a reputation for being easy.

CLEM. Yes.

ONI. Sexually.

CLEM. Yes.

—

ONI. They have sex in bus shelt–

CLEM. I get it.

—

—

Shall we have some tea with the cake I bought?

ONI. Excellent idea.

CLEM. Shall we have it outside?

DAVID. No.

CLEM. I'd like to go out to the birds. I haven't seen the –

ONI. The back door is open, feel free to –

CLEM. I'd like to go out with Dad. We could sit in the garden and have a look with –

DAVID. Wasps.

—

Wasps.

ONI. Ah yes, sorry, I should have said. The wasps. They... He can't... (*Motions batting them away.*)

—

—

I heard you got a job as a wasp-killer.

CLEM. What?

ONI. I heard you got a job as a wasp-killer.

CLEM. Oh right, I see.

—

DAVID. Not proper job.

ONI. It's a real buzz.

DAVID. Not proper job.

ONI. It was a good effort though.

DAVID. No. And wasps no buzz.

ONI. Your father is very pedantic.

CLEM *reaches over and goes on the iPad. She gets up a picture of a scan.*

DAVID. Beekeeper.

ONI. Okay, I got a job as a beekeeper. It was a real buzz.

DAVID. You in it for honey.

—

In it for the honey.

—

The honey.

ONI. Ha. Yes. In it for the honey. Like money. Very good, David, very –

CLEM *shows them the picture*.

Oh, Clementine.

—

She's a beauty.

CLEM. Thank you.

ONI. Look at how she's smiling. David, look.

—

So lovely.

—

So so lovely. A peach. Her tiny little hands.

CLEM. I know, right?

ONI. How long now?

CLEM. Five months.

ONI. So… December.

—

CLEM. We get her on 16th December.

—

ONI. You must be over the moon.

CLEM. We are.

ONI. You must be over the moon and back.

CLEM. Yes.

ONI. And you will be a grandfather.

—

Grandpa David.

—

All the benefits without the backside pain of having them full-time. No offence, Clem.

CLEM. None taken.

ONI. I can't wait for AJ to have babies. I can't wait to hold their fat little hands. Pat their fat little bottoms.

—

—

She's wonderful.

—

—

CLEM *looks at* DAVID.

—

DAVID. Beautiful.

—

CLEM. I can print you a copy if you want.

—

—

ONI. This pattern of your dress is very nice.

CLEM. Thank you. It's only Primark.

ONI. I love Primark.

CLEM. Yeah, some of the stuff is nice. I don't usually –

ONI. My daughter cannot wait to come over to go shopping in Primark.

CLEM. Is she coming soon?

ONI. When we win the Lottery. Okay, so green tea for you. Peppermint for me. And builder's for David, how does that sound?

CLEM. Great. That sounds great –

DAVID *makes a noise. A choking sound.*

ONI. Sometimes the neck brace slips a little and –

ONI *readjusts* DAVID*'s neck brace. Moves* DAVID*'s head in the right position.*

Is that better?

DAVID *groans.*

Is it digging?

—

Oh, yes, I see. Hold on. (*Moves the brace.*)

—

Hold your horses.

—

Better?

DAVID. Yes.

DAVID *coughs again. She moves his head again. It hurts him.* CLEM *watches.*

ONI. Sorry.

DAVID. Okay.

—

ONI. Yes?

DAVID. Yes.

ONI. So, tea?

—

Clem?

—

CLEM. Yes. Please.

ONI *leaves the room.*

Have any other old friends been over?

DAVID. Just Terry.

—

—

CLEM (*gets on computer*). I wanted to show you this.

She goes to YouTube and searches for a clip of zebra finches.

Remember George? And when you used to come home from work, he used to fly on to your shoulder... ah, here we go.

She plays the clip – a zebra finch jumps on the shoulder of a man.

Just like George, isn't he? So sweet. So tame.

She plays it again. They watch. DAVID *presses it again to watch it again.*

I was thinking maybe you'd like a couple of zebra finches to go with the others. And I was looking online and you can order them and have them couriered over. It only takes a couple of days. It's been ages since you had any and they're so pretty.

He watches the clip again.

What do you think?

DAVID *makes a choking/sobbing sound.*

Dad?

—

What is it?

—

Shit. (*Calls.*) Oni, there's something wrong with Dad.

—

(*Shouts.*) Oni!

ONI *comes back into the room. She looks at* DAVID. *He is crying.*

ONI. Oh, David.

ONI *moves to* DAVID *and wipes his tears with her fingers.* CLEM *watches.*

Where's the tissue?

—

Do you –

CLEM. Yes, yes, of course.

CLEM *gets a tissue from her bag.*

—

ONI *wipes* DAVID'*s tears away.*

ONI. He'll be fine in a minute.

—

He gets emotional.

—

Overwhelmed.

DAVID *cries.* ONI *puts her arms around him. She kisses his head. She wipes his nose.* CLEM *watches.*

Come on now. Let it out. That's it.

—

That's it, my darling.

—

That's it.

—

Let it go.

—

Eight

Clem's House

CLEM *and* DAUGHTER. LAKSHMI *is there too.* CLEM *doesn't see/acknowledge her.*

—

DAUGHTER. About the size of this room. Roughly.

CLEM. And how many surrogates are there?

DAUGHTER. Twelve –

LAKSHMI. Fourteen –

DAUGHTER. Something like that.

CLEM. Must get noisy.

DAUGHTER. Sometimes it's so noisy I can hardly hear myself think.

CLEM. Really?

DAUGHTER. There's a lot of laughing.

CLEM. Is there?

DAUGHTER. Put a whole load of women together, there's bound to be.

—

Remember how you used to –

CLEM. Yeah.

DAUGHTER. With Melanie and Justine.

—

That time that Melanie laughed so hard, she was sick.

—

In that Spanish restaurant you all used to go to. What was she laughing about?

CLEM. I don't remember.

DAUGHTER. Yes, you do.

CLEM. Something about a date that ended with her hiding up a tree.

DAUGHTER. Oh yeah. She was hysterical when she was telling you. And then she just puked. And Justine was shouting at her to go to the toilet. And she just kept on puking into her salad and laughing.

CLEM. It was so disgusting.

DAUGHTER. It was so funny.

CLEM. Melanie was always so –

DAUGHTER. When was the last time you saw her?

CLEM. Ages.

DAUGHTER. Did she move abroad?

CLEM. No.

DAUGHTER. I thought she moved to Sydney.

CLEM. No, that was Sonya.

DAUGHTER. After she had her kids, I thought she –

CLEM. No, Melanie's still here.

—

DAUGHTER. How many kids has she –

CLEM. Three.

—

She had another little girl two years ago.

—

Ella.

DAUGHTER. But you haven't –

CLEM. No.

DAUGHTER. You've never –

CLEM. No.

—

So the women like it there?

DAUGHTER. Yeah, most do. They're getting regular food and
they like hanging out with each other.

CLEM. That's good.

DAUGHTER. And they all enjoy the lack of responsibility.

—

What I mean is they don't have to get up at 4 a.m. and work
sixteen hours in some fucking sweatshop somewhere and
then shop and cook dinner and clean and look after kids and
husbands and in-laws and deal with all that shit.

—

They're being taken care of.

CLEM. Yeah.

DAUGHTER. Probably more than they've ever been taken care of before.

—

—

There's this malt drink they're given. It's disgusting. Full of vitamins. Good for the –

LAKSHMI. – babies –

DAUGHTER. – and all that, but tastes like a kind of mouldy chalky yogurt. They hate it. They are all united in their hatred of the drink.

CLEM. Apart from the drink, it sounds –

DAUGHTER. There's quite a lot of arguing because they're so young.

CLEM. They're not that young.

DAUGHTER. And when the woman died, everything was pretty horrible.

—

There was a weird atmosphere for ages after that.

—

She was seven months pregnant.

—

She'd been quiet for a few days, but no one had really noticed, because, well, sometimes the women go quiet. She went to bed and in the night, she started –

LAKSHMI. Screaming.

DAUGHTER. Then they took her away. Her bed was covered in –

LAKSHMI. – blood.

—

DAUGHTER. The baby survived if that's what you're
    wondering.

CLEM. I wasn't wondering –

DAUGHTER. Sorry, I thought you –

CLEM. No.

    —

    —

DAUGHTER. The parents are from New York. He's a foreign
    correspondent. She's a lawyer.

    —

    You don't have to worry. Your surrogate is healthy.

CLEM. Lakshmi.

    —

DAUGHTER. Lakshmi is healthy.

    —

    —

CLEM. What does she know about us?

    —

    About Daddy and me?

DAUGHTER. Nothing much.

    —

    The minimum. Enough.

    —

CLEM. How does she feel about us?

    —

    When she thinks about me, what does she –

DAUGHTER. She doesn't really think about you.

CLEM. Doesn't she?

DAUGHTER. She thinks about me.

CLEM. Okay. Good.

—

And what does she feel about you?

LAKSHMI. Nothing.

DAUGHTER. She's not a fool. She knows I'm yours.

CLEM. But –

DAUGHTER. She's protective of me. But –

LAKSHMI. It's business.

DAUGHTER. You can't have it both ways. You can't want her to love me and not love me as well.

CLEM. No, I know, but –

DAUGHTER. And she has her own children to think about.

CLEM. Yes, of course.

DAUGHTER. She worries about them.

—

She worries that something will happen to them because she's not there.

CLEM. They're with their father.

DAUGHTER. She's anxious, that's all.

CLEM. He's taking care of them.

DAUGHTER. She's away from them and she's anxious. You'd be the same.

—

—

—

CLEM. What's she doing right now?

DAUGHTER. She's lying on her bed dreaming of –

LAKSHMI. – home.

—

DAUGHTER. She's kissing her son's forehead.

—

Plaiting her daughter's hair.

—

She's holding them tight to her chest.

LAKSHMI. Inhaling them.

DAUGHTER. Holding them tighter than anyone has ever held a child before.

Nine

Clem's House/David's House Skype

CLEM *and* DAVID *skyping*.

CLEM. We've decided to call her Megan.

—

We both agree. We want to call her Megan.

—

Can you hear me? Megan, like Mum.

DAVID. Yes

CLEM. I thought maybe you couldn't, because…

DAVID. I hear you.

—

CLEM. What do you think?

DAVID. Okay.

CLEM. Okay?

DAVID. Your decision.

—

—

CLEM. Did you go to the group?

—

The support group.

—

The one I told you about.

DAVID. No.

—

CLEM. Why didn't you –

—

I could go with you, if you like. There's an evening session,
I think. Next week I could… I'm free next week on Tuesday,
so…

—

Or maybe one of the evening people could go with you if
you'd prefer.

—

The medical team suggested it, didn't they?

—

Audrey said that –

DAVID. Yes.

CLEM. Audrey said it was often helpful to meet others who –

DAVID. It's not a club.

—

Nothing in common.

—

Unlucky bastards. That's it.

—

Useless unlucky bastards.

CLEM. It would be good for you to have someone to talk to. Someone who understands.

JOSH (*calling*). Have you seen my –

JOSH *walks in*.

CLEM. I'm talking to Dad.

JOSH (*mouths*). Sorry.

CLEM. Come and say hello.

Goes round to the screen.

JOSH. Hi, David.

DAVID. Hi.

JOSH. Good to see you getting on with modern technology at last.

DAVID. Yes.

JOSH. How's the laptop working out for you?

DAVID. Yes. Thank you.

JOSH. I didn't mean… No need for… It suits you…

—

How are you?

—

Obviously not great, but you know… how are things generally –

CLEM. I was telling Dad about calling the baby Megan.

JOSH. Right. Brilliant. Do you approve?

—

We were talking for ages about what to call her and then in a flash it just hit Clem.

CLEM. Seems so obvious now.

—

—

JOSH. You been following the season?

DAVID. No.

JOSH. None of it?

DAVID. No

—

JOSH. You're not missing much. It's been shit.

CLEM. Don't start on that. (*To* DAVID.) You should see the moping about. It's pathetic.

JOSH. She doesn't get it, does she, David? She'll never get it.

—

—

Well, I've got a ton of work I need to do, so I'll let you… Great to see you, David.

CLEM (*to* JOSH). What were you looking for?

JOSH. My charger. I thought it was –

CLEM. Bedroom floor.

JOSH *goes*.

—

How are you getting on with the evening people?

—

I thought Jimmy seemed nice. And Evka too. She seems very on top of things.

—

She was telling me in the Czech Republic that she used to be a primary schoolteacher.

—

Is that right?

DAVID. Don't know.

CLEM. Don't you speak to her?

—

Why don't you call her, so I can say hello?

—

Dad, can you –

DAVID. No.

—

CLEM. If you don't like her, I can call the agency and ask them to send someone else. If that's –

DAVID. How is Lakshmi?

—

Lakshmi? How is –

CLEM. Fine. She's fine. Everything's fine.

—

Everything is as it should be.

—

The baby is really growing. I mean Megan. Can't get used to her having a name. Megan is really growing. All fit and healthy.

—

The clinic sends us updates every week. We Skyped at first, but the agency isn't keen on that. It can be stressful so they don't encourage it and to be honest, it was… Anyway she's fine. Everything is going to plan.

DAVID. Your mother hated her name.

CLEM. What?

DAVID. Megan. Hated her name.

—

Hated it.

CLEM. That's not true. Mum never said she –

DAVID. She did.

CLEM. Why are you saying that?

DAVID. True.

—

CLEM. Did she really –

DAVID. Yes.

—

—

—

CLEM. Did you finish listening to *Bleak House*?

—

—

Dad, did you finish it?

DAVID *lurches out of view.*

I can't see you properly. You've…

—

Dad, can you straighten the…

—

Or sit to the left…

—

Call Evka and she can –

—

Call Evka.

DAVID. No.

CLEM. Call her and she can –

DAVID. Can't stand this.

CLEM. What?

DAVID. Can't stand it.

CLEM. Call her.

DAVID. Strangers.

—

In house.

—

Can't stand it.

—

Strangers in my house.

CLEM. I thought you wanted to stay in the house.

—

That's what you said. That's what you've always said. We're trying to keep you at home, because you said that –

DAVID. Hate it.

—

Touching my skin.

—

Invading me.

—

Making me feel…

—

—

Had enough.

CLEM. Don't say that. It's –

DAVID. Enough.

CLEM. You've still got things you can enjoy.

DAVID. Like what?

—

What?

—

CLEM. What will happen to your birds if you…

DAVID. I want to –

CLEM. Don't say it, Daddy. Please don't say it.

DAVID. Suffocating.

—

Drowning

—

Every night. Fucking drowning.

CLEM. It's alright.

DAVID. Not alright.

CLEM. Everything will be –

DAVID. Nothing alright.

CLEM. We can get more help. Me and Josh can pay for –

DAVID. You.

CLEM. What?

DAVID. You.

—

—

CLEM. Oh, Dad, I can't.

DAVID. You.

CLEM. The baby's coming soon and –

DAVID. You.

CLEM. It's just not feasible for us to –

DAVID. Ashamed.

CLEM. And we're both working flat-out to –

DAVID. Ashamed.

CLEM. What?

DAVID. Of you.

—

I ashamed of you.

—

Ten

David's House

CLEM *at the front door.* ONI *stands in her path.*

ONI. I'm sorry, but –

CLEM. Just for a minute.

ONI. I am really very –

CLEM. But –

ONI. I can't.

—

CLEM. Please.

ONI. Clem, go home.

—

It's better if you go home.

—

You have to respect his wishes.

—

I told you, he doesn't want to –

CLEM. I need to speak to him.

ONI. You have to be patient.

CLEM. I've been patient.

—

ONI. I'll phone you when he's ready.

CLEM. If I could just –

ONI. He doesn't want to.

—

CLEM. What right have you to –

ONI. I'm following his instructions.

CLEM. You have no right to… I'm his next of kin.

—

ONI. I have to go.

> CLEM *puts her foot in the door.*

Please take your –

—

I'm doing what he's asked me, I'm –

CLEM (*calls*). Dad. Dad.

> ONI *steps aside.* CLEM *goes into the living room.* DAVID *sits.* ONI *follows* CLEM *in.*

If it was possible then we'd do it.

—

If it was in any way possible then we would…

—

You know that, don't you?

—

But with the baby coming, it's just not… I'm too far away and…

—

I can't care for you. It would be wrong of me to say that I could.

—

If I could, I would.

—

You know that.

—

But you've got Oni and she's brilliant and the other carers are good too, aren't they?

—

Aren't they?

—

ONI *goes to leave the room*.

DAVID. Stay.

—

CLEM. You wouldn't want to live with Josh anyway. You wouldn't want to.

—

Would you?

—

Would you want to live with – ?

DAVID. No.

CLEM. Of course you wouldn't. I know that. So this is all... What? What is this?

—

—

I know it's hard. It's really bloody hard. I understand. And I'll do everything I can to make it better. I will, I promise, but –

DAVID. Go home.

—

DAVID. Go.

CLEM. But –

DAVID. Don't want.

—

Don't want.

CLEM. I thought you –

DAVID. Make me sick.

ONI. David…

DAVID. Go.

—

Now.

ONI. You should probably –

DAVID. So ashamed.

—

You.

—

My blood.

CLEM. I've explained. I can't just –

DAVID (*to* ONI). Ask her.

—

(*To* ONI.) Ask.

ONI (*to* DAVID). No, David.

DAVID. Ask.

CLEM. Ask me what?

DAVID. Ask.

CLEM. What? What is it?

DAVID. Please.

—

—

ONI. He wants to know if you knew that in Russia the surrogate is protected.

—

David wants to know if you knew that in Russia the surrogate has legal rights.

CLEM. Why does he –

ONI. But in India, the surrogate has no rights.

—

Lakshmi has no protection. No one is looking out for her.

—

He wants to know if you knew this. When you chose your surrogate, did you know?

—

—

—

—

I have things to do. Excuse me.

ONI *leaves*.

—

—

—

—

—

—

—

—

CLEM. Do you have any idea what it's like not being able to have a child?

—

—

It's awful.

—

—

The pain is… the pain of it is…

—

—

—

I can't escape it. Everywhere I look. Everyone I know.
Everyone I meet has children. It's impossible to… it feels
so… It's impossible. And they always ask me if I have any.
I cannot get away from that question. And when I say no, they
don't know what to do, because it's… it feels… I watch them
search about where to go next, is it okay for them to carry on
talking about their kids or should they find something else to
talk about? And then they decide it'll look worse if they
change the subject, so they carry on about Lola's art class or
Harry's option choices or the family holiday in Cornwall as if
I give a shit. And the more they talk, the more they know who
they are, what they are part of; their unit, their little gang.
They are so certain of why they are here.

I'm a mother. What are you?

Then they see me fading away and start complaining about
how rude Joseph is, how Tilly is being bullied and Maisie is
out of control and how tiring it all is, never having a moment
to yourself, an inverse to all the positives. It's pity and we
both know it. And I fucking hate them for it. Not having a
child makes me hate everyone who does.

—

—

—

—

—

When you have one of your own everything shifts. That's what they say. You recalibrate. Your world view completely changes, because of the love you feel for your child. The overwhelming, all-consuming, undeniable –

DAVID. She's not your child.

—

—

—

—

—

CLEM. I wake up every morning with this ache, with this gnawing feeling of loss and displacement and horror that this is it for me. This is all my life will ever be.

—

Is that what you want?

—

Is it?

—

Is that what you want for me?

—

Say something.

—

Speak.

—

Speak.

—

Fucking speak.

—

Eleven

Clem's House

CLEM *and* DAUGHTER. LAKSHMI *is there.*

DAUGHTER. I hate my art teacher. She's a total cunt.

CLEM. Whoa. What's with the C-bomb?

DAUGHTER. Why are you calling it that? As if you don't say cunt.

CLEM. Actually. I don't think I do say –

DAUGHTER. Yes, you do. When you think I'm not listening.

CLEM. Still, it's not very nice to call your teacher –

DAUGHTER. All she ever does is moan. I wish I'd never taken art.

CLEM. You're good at art.

DAUGHTER. I should have taken music instead.

CLEM. You're great at music.

DAUGHTER. Do you think so?

CLEM. Yes.

DAUGHTER. You're terrible at music.

CLEM. Yup. What? No, I don't think that's –

DAUGHTER. And Daddy is just about the worst singer I've ever heard.

CLEM. He's not that bad.

DAUGHTER. What's that song he always sings?

CLEM. Happy Mondays.

DAUGHTER. Happy Mondays. Sad bastard.

CLEM. Your father is not a sad bastard. He is –

DAUGHTER *sings the third line from 'Step On' by the Happy Mondays.* CLEM *sings the fourth. They both sing the refrain.*

DAUGHTER *and* LAKSHMI *sing the refrain in Hindi.*

Not funny.

DAUGHTER *sings the refrain in Russian.*

CLEM. Still not funny.

DAUGHTER. Why do you want to be a mother?

CLEM. Why does any woman want to be a mother?

DAUGHTER. I don't know. I don't.

CLEM. You will.

DAUGHTER. I won't.

CLEM. You'll change your mind.

DAUGHTER. No, I don't think so.

CLEM. Really, you'll –

DAUGHTER. No.

—

CLEM. When you meet the right person.

—

When you meet the right person and all you can think about is how much you want to have a child with them.

DAUGHTER. Is that how you felt about Daddy?

CLEM. I thought I was going to explode if I didn't.

DAUGHTER. You imagined her with his mouth.

CLEM. Yes.

DAUGHTER. You wanted her to have his laugh. But you wanted her to have your eyes.

—

You used to lie in bed and look at each other, couldn't
believe that you'd found each other.

–

Do I have his laugh?

CLEM. Yes.

DAUGHTER. Do I have his mouth?

–

–

When I was in the womb of the child surrogate, she –

CLEM. She's wasn't a – She isn't a child. And she's called –

DAUGHTER. How old is she?

CLEM. Twenty-three.

DAUGHTER. She seems younger. She doesn't have any shoes.

CLEM. Not everyone wears shoes in India.

–

DAUGHTER. I could feel that she wasn't wearing shoes.

–

I could feel the –

LAKSHMI. – heat –

DAUGHTER. – on the soles of her feet. The –

LAKSHMI. – rub –

DAUGHTER. – of the –

LAKSHMI. – grit –

DAUGHTER. – when she ran.

CLEM. Ran where?

DAUGHTER. She was –

LAKSHMI. – running –

DAUGHTER. – through the –

LAKSHMI. – streets –

DAUGHTER. – so fast and –

LAKSHMI. – pushing

DAUGHTER. – people out of the way –

LAKSHMI. – shouting –

DAUGHTER. – at them to move –

CLEM. But why was she running?

DAUGHTER. Because she had to get –

LAKSHMI. – home.

CLEM. She's not allowed to go home.

DAUGHTER. Sweat –

LAKSHMI. – pouring –

DAUGHTER. Her whole body –

LAKSHMI. – drenched.

DAUGHTER. Her heart –

LAKSHMI. – pounding –

DAUGHTER. – out of her chest.

CLEM. She's not allowed to leave the centre.

DAUGHTER. She broke a window, opened the door from the outside.

—

A piece of glass got stuck in the soft part of her foot, the pad, but she was so –

LAKSHMI. – frantic –

DAUGHTER. She didn't even –

LAKSHMI. – notice.

CLEM. Why –

DAUGHTER. Thinking about her kids all alone and –

CLEM. They're not alone.

DAUGHTER. And how they are coping without her.

CLEM. Her husband is –

DAUGHTER. He's not there.

CLEM. What?

DAUGHTER. He's not there.

CLEM. Where is he?

—

Where is he?

DAUGHTER. I don't know.

—

Out working maybe. Or… I don't know.

—

—

The glass is still there. In her foot. She can't put too much pressure on it. The pain shoots straight up her. Pierces her –

LAKSHMI. – heart.

Twelve

Clem's House/Fertility Clinic Skype

—

JOSH. You knew.

DR SHARMA. I can assure you that we did not –

JOSH. How could you not?

DR SHARMA. We found out yesterday.

JOSH. This is your field. Your area of expertise. You must have –

DR SHARMA. We were given instruction yesterday. The government gave instruction yester–

JOSH. Bullshit.

DR SHARMA. I appreciate that you are feeling –

JOSH. Absolute bullshit.

—

DR SHARMA. Mr Kennedy-Clarke, we were told yesterday. All the agencies were told –

JOSH. You stitched us up.

—

DR SHARMA. I do not know what that means.

JOSH. It means you knew that this was going to happen.

DR SHARMA. No, we –

JOSH. And you decided to take our money and cross your fingers and hope for the fucking best.

DR SHARMA. I can assure you that –

JOSH. You can't assure us of anything. If one thing has become clear, it's that.

—

DR SHARMA. I understand how this –

JOSH. You do not understand.

DR SHARMA. I understand that you must be –

JOSH. Stop saying that.

DR SHARMA. But –

JOSH. Stop bloody saying it.

—

DR SHARMA. No one anticipated this.

JOSH. You must have known that –

DR SHARMA. It's very disappointing that –

JOSH. A ban was imminent.

—

DR SHARMA. Surrogacy has not been banned.

JOSH. It's illegal.

DR SHARMA. No, they have said we cannot take on any more foreign clients.

—

We have been instructed not to take any more foreign clients.

There's no more detail than that.

JOSH. And what about us? What are we supposed to do?

—

What about our baby?

DR SHARMA. Nothing has been stated about surrogacy that is already underway.

JOSH. How can that be? How can they declare a ban and not say anything about people like us?

DR SHARMA. We will know all the details when they have drafted the bill.

JOSH. When will that be?

DR SHARMA. We do not know.

JOSH. This is…

—

This is so…

DR SHARMA. We do not have the information you want, but I think we can assume that those mid-process will be protected. I should not be saying it, because we have had no instruction, but it is what we anticipate.

JOSH. Okay… So… okay…

DR SHARMA. We have many other clients in exactly the same situation as yourselves. Our legal team is trying to find out the details as we speak. We are doing everything we can to find out exactly –

CLEM. Does Lakshmi know?

DR SHARMA. All the surrogates have been informed.

CLEM. And she's been sent home?

JOSH (*to* CLEM). What?

DR SHARMA. No, she has not been sent home.

CLEM. Lakshmi hasn't left the centre?

DR SHARMA. No, none of the surrogates have left.

CLEM. Are you sure, because –

DR SHARMA. Yes, they are all still with us.

JOSH. And what do you suggest we do now?

DR SHARMA. We just have to wait. As soon as we –

CLEM. And you've definitely told her?

JOSH (*to* CLEM). Why are you –

CLEM. You've told Lakshmi about the new rule?

DR SHARMA. All the ladies have been told. Obviously, this is very upsetting for them, but we have reassured them as best we can that –

JOSH. Well, I'm glad you've reassured them.

DR SHARMA. I understand how hard this is for you both. I do. And the not knowing exactly what is happening is agonising, but you will be okay. Honestly, I think –

JOSH. Honestly?

–

DR SHARMA. The baby is genetically yours, Mr Kennedy-Clarke. You are her father. There can be no stronger argument than that.

–

JOSH. We're going to fly over.

DR SHARMA. There is no need.

JOSH. We need to be there. We need to –

DR SHARMA. There's nothing you can do here. We have to wait.

JOSH. But –

DR SHARMA. Stay where you are. I promise you, as soon as I know anything I will contact you straight away.

–

And please, I know this is difficult, but you must try not to worry.

–

I have to go now.

JOSH. But –

DR SHARMA. Goodbye, Mr Kennedy-Clarke.

JOSH. But –

DR SHARMA. Goodbye.

She goes.

JOSH. Fuck.

—

This is so fucking…

—

Fuck.

—

She must have known this was coming. She must have. How could she not?

—

What sort of government makes a decision and implements it overnight with no thought about the consequences?

—

Those bastards.

—

How can they do this?

—

This is so unbelievably fucked. That stupid fucking country.

—

They can't keep her. Legally, there's no way that they can keep her from us.

—

I will not allow that to happen.

CLEM. What does Lakshmi's husband do?

—

What does he do for a living?

JOSH. What?

CLEM. Did we ever find that out?

JOSH. Why are –

CLEM. Were we told? Did the agency ever –

JOSH. What does it –

CLEM. Who's looking after her kids when he's out working?

—

He still has to go to work, so what are her kids doing while he's away?

—

What do we know about –

JOSH. Stop.

CLEM. What do we actually know about –

JOSH. Stop it.

CLEM. Why didn't we –

JOSH. Enough.

CLEM. We should have –

JOSH. Don't.

CLEM. But –

JOSH. Everything is going to be okay. You heard Dr Sharma.

—

She said it.

—

There's no need to panic. I'm sorry if I've made you…
There's no need to panic.

—

We're going to get our baby and we're going to bring her back here just like we planned. Megan will come home and we'll have the family you've always wanted. I promise.

—

Thirteen

Clem's House

DAUGHTER *is working on a sketchbook. She shows her drawing to* CLEM. LAKSHMI *is present.*

DAUGHTER. That's my mother.

CLEM. Lakshmi is not your mother.

DAUGHTER. I know. (*Points at drawing.*) She's the surrogate, that's why she's over there.

—

What's my mother's name?

CLEM. I'm your mother.

DAUGHTER. Did you go to Russia to meet her?

—

Did you pick her out of a book, a database or something? Was it because she was pretty? Or clever? Was it because she was tall? Tall people are the most successful. They're the ones that are all CEOs of big companies and stuff. They can pull the berries off the trees while everyone else is still jumping up. What's her name?

CLEM. I don't know.

DAUGHTER. What part of Russia is she from?

CLEM. I don't know.

DAUGHTER. Does she have any children?

CLEM. Stop asking me.

—

DAUGHTER. When I was being born, Lakshmi tried to pull me out herself. Her fingernails scraped the top of my head. They shouted at her. They shouted that she'd already broken her contract once when she ran away.

CLEM. She didn't run away.

DAUGHTER. I've got a scar where she pulled my ear. Look.

CLEM. She hasn't left the centre.

DAUGHTER. I didn't want to come out. They brought me out early.

—

They thought I was in danger.

—

They thought I was in –

CLEM. You weren't in danger. You are not in –

DAUGHTER. I'm illegal.

—

They've made me illegal.

CLEM. You're not illegal.

DAUGHTER. That's what it feels like.

—

What's going to happen?

CLEM. We've got lawyers.

DAUGHTER. Have we?

CLEM. It will be okay.

DAUGHTER. Will it?

CLEM. Yes.

—

DAUGHTER. Why did they do that?

—

All those poor couples with no children and no hope.

CLEM. Politics.

DAUGHTER. Is it because they think the surrogates are victims? That they can't make decisions about how to use their own bodies without government intervention.

CLEM. Exactly. It's just pandering –

DAUGHTER. To people who know fuck-all about it.

CLEM. Yes. It's pathetic –

DAUGHTER. And patronising.

CLEM. To think they have –

DAUGHTER. No free will.

CLEM. That they are hav–

DAUGHTER. No choice.

CLEM. It's not a moral issue.

DAUGHTER. I know. If it was a moral issue –

CLEM. They would have banned surrogacy.

DAUGHTER. For everyone.

CLEM. Not just the foreigners.

DAUGHTER. If anything it's worse for the surrogates –

CLEM. It just means less money.

DAUGHTER. Same job –

LAKSHMI. Less money.

—

CLEM. Lakshmi will be okay.

DAUGHTER. She'll get her money.

CLEM. And it will change her life.

DAUGHTER. Get her a –

LAKSHMI. Home.

CLEM. And a business.

DAUGHTER. Send her –

LAKSHMI. – son and daughter –

DAUGHTER. – to school.

CLEM. And it will all be worth it.

DAUGHTER. Are you sure?

CLEM. Yes.

—

—

DAUGHTER. Where will they go?

CLEM. Who?

DAUGHTER. The poor couples with no hope and no children.

CLEM. I don't know.

DAUGHTER. They'll find somewhere.

—

A different poor country.

—

LAKSHMI. When one door shuts another one opens.

—

DAUGHTER. Were you there when I was born?

CLEM. Yes.

DAUGHTER. I don't remember you –

CLEM. I was there.

DAUGHTER. Daddy held me first. I remember that.

—

And the doctor told Lakshmi to stop calling me that name.

—

She had a name for me.

—

The doctor was angry with her.

—

She wouldn't stop saying it.

—

The doctor put a hand over her mouth to shut her up.

—

Do you know the name?

—

LAKSHMI (*Hindi*). *Kavva*.

—

DAUGHTER. Do you know what that means?

—

Do you want to know?

—

Why not?

—

LAKSHMI. Crow.

—

DAUGHTER. She called me Crow.

Fourteen

Clem's House

Living room. ONI *wearing her coat.* CLEM *stands.*

CLEM. Would you like a –

ONI. I'm okay.

CLEM. Are you sure, because I can easily –

ONI. Really.

CLEM. It's no bother –

ONI. No, thank you.

—

CLEM. How did you get here?

ONI. I drove.

CLEM. How long did it take you?

ONI. About an hour and twenty minutes.

CLEM. That's pretty good. Sometimes it takes me two hours.
    Once it was three, but that was because of the rugby.

—

    What do you drive?

ONI. A Nissan Micra.

CLEM. Is it good?

—

ONI. Yes.

CLEM. Is it reliable?

ONI. Yes.

CLEM. Our old next-door neighbour had one, went on and on about it being reliable, that's why I said that.

ONI. It's very reliable. Looks like shit, but it's very reliable.

—

CLEM. Please. Let me… (*Goes to take* ONI*'s coat.*)

ONI. Actually, I'm a bit cold.

CLEM. I can turn the heating on. We don't normally… until eight… we monitor our energy use… Josh is very… I mean we both are… we don't… I'll put it on. I'll just… Fuck it… I'll –

ONI. I can keep my coat –

CLEM. No really, it's… That's ridiculous, I'll just…

She puts on the heating.

I've been working on this new series. It's a complete nightmare. No one's got a clue what they're doing. And I haven't been feeling very well, so I've had to do a lot of it from home, which, as you can imagine is… Well, it doesn't matter. It's not important. Are you sure I can't get you –

ONI. Okay, I'll have a tea.

CLEM. Great. Okay. Great. What sort would you like?

ONI. Normal.

CLEM. Milk, sugar?

ONI. Just milk.

CLEM. Just milk. Normal tea. Right. Coming right up.

CLEM *goes. A while. She comes back.*

We haven't got any milk. I've got soya or loads of herbal teas if you'd prefer. I think there's a peppermint if you –

ONI. You need to come and see him.

—

CLEM. I've been really busy, what with work and everything. It's all been pretty –

ONI. He's really not very well.

—

CLEM. I get the reports.

—

I know what's going on for him. I organise all of that. You know that, don't you?

—

You know that a large proportion of my time is negotiating with the agency getting people in and out of the house so he's not alone and making sure that he's at hospital appointments and there's someone to go with him and report back to me about what's been said and what needs to happen next. And all the while trying to keep him comfortable and supported.

ONI. Yes.

CLEM. I spend more than fifty per cent of my time organising his care. It's not as if I'm not doing anything and I don't know what's going on. I know exactly what's happening, but I do have a job and I do have a baby on the way as well, so…

ONI. You're busy. I understand.

—

—

—

CLEM. I think it's really quite rude of you to come here and
start…

—

I think it's…

—

Who's with him now if you're…

ONI. Celia this morning. Evka this afternoon. George tonight.

—

—

—

His speech is almost entirely –

CLEM. I know.

ONI. Soon he won't be able to –

CLEM. Yes. I know.

—

—

—

What's he been doing?

ONI. Listening to the books, watching television, but he thinks
it's all rubbish. Yesterday I got some of his records from the
loft and we played them.

CLEM. What did you play?

ONI. The Rolling Stones.

—

CLEM. Did he say he liked The Stones?

ONI. Yes.

CLEM. What did he say about Mick Jagger?

—

What did he say about –

ONI. Nothing.

CLEM. Which album did you play?

—

What did it look like?

—

Did it have a cake on the front? Like a big layered birthday cake or something? Did it have…

ONI. Clem…

CLEM. He hates The Stones. He's always hated them. It was Mum that loved them. Dad was a Beatles man. There's probably loads of Beatles albums up there. You should get those down for him.

ONI. Why don't you come round and play them to him?

—

Or you could Skype him.

—

I can sit with him and help. I could do that tomorrow evening. I could ask him if he'd like to do that and then text you.

—

—

—

CLEM. Does he know you're here?

ONI. No.

CLEM. What do you think he'd say if he knew?

ONI. He'd be pissed off. He's a stubborn old goat.

CLEM. Yeah, he is.

ONI. Maybe it's genetic.

—

—

—

CLEM. What's he said about me?

—

—

—

ONI. He loves you.

CLEM. Does he?

ONI. You know he does.

—

—

You can't expect him to change who he is. It's not fair.

—

—

—

CLEM. Why are you here?

—

What difference does it make to you?

—

Seriously, why are you…?

—

You've travelled all the way here on your day off, for what?

ONI. Your father needs you.

CLEM. I've got a baby coming.

—

—

In two weeks I have to go to India to collect the baby.

ONI. Yes.

—

And my understanding is that things have become more complicated for you all.

—

—

CLEM. It's under control.

ONI. Is it?

CLEM. Everything is under control.

—

They're reviewing everyone case by case. We'll be interviewed by the immigration people in India and then we'll get the exit visas. And then we'll all come home.

ONI. I see.

CLEM. There are people over there with embryos who will never get a child, because they didn't start the process early enough. If anything we're the lucky ones. It doesn't feel like it, but we are.

—

—

—

ONI. And how long will you be in India?

—

CLEM. They're saying about two months. Two months at the very most.

—

ONI. You need to see him before you go.

—

—

—

CLEM. Does he know?

—

—

Does he know about the change in the –

ONI. Yes.

—

—

—

Don't miss your chance, Clem. Not when you don't have to.

—

—

—

CLEM. I can't.

—

I'm sorry.

—

I can't.

—

—

Fifteen

Clem's House

CLEM *is packing*. DAUGHTER *and* LAKSHMI *are there*.

DAUGHTER. What part of me belongs to you?

—

Which bits of me are yours? I can tell you exactly what's
Daddy's. The maths, the jokes, the spatial awareness and the
art stuff.

—

When are you going to tell me? Right from the start so it's
not a shock? Or when you think I'm old enough to
understand? Or maybe you'll let me find out myself by
accident when I need my birth certificate. You know, bury
the landmine and wait for me to stumble on it.

—

You must have thought about how it will affect me.

—

You must have.

—

I'm trying to help you. Because I'll want to know. I'll want
to know why I don't look you. And why I don't act like you.
Or think like you or feel like you. Why I feel a million miles
away from you when you're supposed to be my mother. I'll
look at you and I won't know who I am.

—

Who am I?

—

Look at me.

—

Are you more like your mum or your dad?

—

I said are you –

CLEM. That's enough.

DAUGHTER. Why?

CLEM. Because I say so.

DAUGHTER. I think you're a daddy's girl like me.

CLEM. Stop it.

DAUGHTER. But maybe not, because –

CLEM. I'm warning you.

DAUGHTER. If you were a daddy's girl –

CLEM. Go to your room.

DAUGHTER. Then you never would have –

CLEM. Shut up.

DAUGHTER. Bought me.

—

CLEM. Get out.

—

DAUGHTER. Okay.

—

If that's what you want.

DAUGHTER *goes. Silence.*

—

—

—

—

CLEM (*calls*). Megan.

—

(*Calls.*) I didn't mean it.

—

(*Calls.*) Megan.

—

(*Calls.*) Please.

DAUGHTER *appears*.

I'm sorry. I didn't –

DAUGHTER. I know.

CLEM. Thank you.

—

DAUGHTER. You should take a hat.

—

You definitely need a hat. You'll burn to a crisp.

—

Have you got one?

CLEM *pulls out a hat, puts it on.*

Maybe not that hat.

CLEM (*laughs*). What's wrong with this –

DAUGHTER. If you have to ask…

CLEM. You try it.

DAUGHTER. No.

CLEM. Try it. Go on. YOLO.

DAUGHTER. No.

CLEM *tries to put it on her. She laughs.*

Get that monstrosity away from me.

CLEM *chases her.*

Get off me.

CLEM *catches her and puts it on her. They laugh.*

A small Indian BOY *appears at the doorway. About seven years old.*

BOY (*Hindi*). *Aapney Meri bahen ko dekha hai?* [Have you seen my sister?]

—

Mayn apni bahen ko talash kar raha hun. [I'm looking for my sister.]

—

Aapney Meri bahen ko dekha hai? [Have you seen my sister?]

DAUGHTER. He's looking for his sister. She's lost.

—

He's Lakshmi's son.

CLEM. Why did you bring him here?

DAUGHTER. I didn't.

CLEM. Tell him to go.

—

BOY (*Hindi*). *Aapney meri bahen ko dekha hai?* [Have you seen my sister?]

—

CLEM. Tell him to go to his father.

—

Tell him to –

DAUGHTER (*Hindi*). *Apney Bapu kay pass jao.* [Go to your father.]

BOY (*Hindi*). *Mera Bapu mar gaya hai.* [My father is dead.]

DAUGHTER. His father is dead.

CLEM. No, his father is –

DAUGHTER. He died just after the daughter was born.

CLEM. Both Lakshmi's children are being looked after by their father.

—

I know that the children are being looked after by their –

DAUGHTER. Lakshmi's on her own.

CLEM. No, her husband is –

DAUGHTER. She's on her own. That's why she needs the money.

CLEM. She needs the money for a business, to send the children to school, not because –

DAUGHTER. She's a widow.

CLEM. The agency said that she –

BOY (*Hindi*). *Mayn aapni bahen ko talash kar raha hun.* [I'm looking for my sister.]

CLEM. The agency said –

LAKSHMI. That was a lie.

—

—

—

—

CLEM. Tell him I can't help him.

DAUGHTER (*Hindi*). *Yeh teri madad nahin kar sakti.* [She can't help you.]

CLEM. Tell him to go back to whoever is looking after him.

DAUGHTER. No one is looking after him.

CLEM. Somebody must be –

DAUGHTER. He's been looking after his sister.

LAKSHMI. And no one's been looking after him.

CLEM. There must be relatives or –

LAKSHMI. No.

CLEM. Friends or –

LAKSHMI. No.

CLEM. The community. Other villagers who –

LAKSHMI. There's no one.

DAUGHTER. She left her son and her daughter alone.

CLEM. She didn't.

—

She wouldn't.

—

I know that she wouldn't –

DAUGHTER. How do you know?

LAKSHMI. The night before I went to the centre, I tied a piece of string around my daughter's wrist and the other end I gave to my son to hold. I asked him to promise that he would not let go of his little sister until I returned. And for many months, he held on tight. All day and all night. (*Speaks to* BOY.) She slept by your side. And when my daughter called for me, you warmed her heart and soothed her back to her dreams. And in the morning, you washed the sleep from her eyelashes and you plaited her hair into a thick rope down her back. You kept her safe. You held her heart like a small bird. And when she cried for me, you made her laugh and the pain in her lungs disappeared. (*To* CLEM.) They found nuggets of happiness where they could. (*To* BOY.) You would throw her into the air light as a seed. And she would laugh and she would laugh and she would laugh. (*To* CLEM.) But one day, my son wanted to play cricket. His friends were calling for him and he thought it would do no harm. Just for a little bit.

He told his little sister to stand by a tree and wait for him. He let go of the string. He played for eight minutes and when he went back to get her, my daughter was gone.

The BOY *leaves.*

—

CLEM. Is that why she ran away from the centre?

DAUGHTER. I don't know. Ask her.

CLEM. Because she'd heard her daughter was missing –

DAUGHTER. Ask her.

CLEM. You said Lakshmi was worried about her –

DAUGHTER. Ask her.

—

Ask her.

—

CLEM. Is that why you ran away from the –

LAKSHMI. No.

CLEM. Because you heard your daughter was –

LAKSHMI. I ran away from the centre before that happened.

CLEM. I don't understand.

LAKSHMI. I ran away before my son played cricket.

CLEM. I don't und–

DAUGHTER. Listen.

LAKSHMI. I ran away before my daughter was left by the tree.

CLEM. But if you weren't looking for your daughter –

DAUGHTER. Stop talking –

CLEM. – then why did you –

DAUGHTER. Stop –

CLEM. – run away from the –

LAKSHMI. Listen to me.

—

I ran away because I knew something terrible was going to happen.

—

I ran away because I did not want her inside me any more.

—

I ran away because I knew she was illegal.

CLEM. But Dr Sharma said –

LAKSHMI. I ran away because I did not want to look after her.

CLEM. Dr Sharma said –

LAKSHMI. I ran away because I was not going to get my money.

CLEM. Dr Sharma –

DAUGHTER. Laskhmi knew it would all go to shit. Just like your dad knew it would all go to shit, because how could it not?

LAKSHMI. I had to try to stop it. I had to try to stop the bad luck. Stop the bad luck that was coming at me like a hurricane. I could not bear to wait one minute longer. This bad omen inside me growing and growing and growing. I knew something terrible was going to happen. That I would have her –

DAUGHTER. – scratching –

LAKSHMI. – around me for the rest of my life.

DAUGHTER. Clawing –

LAKSHMI. – at my skin.

DAUGHTER. Screeching –

LAKSHMI. – for more food. Her –

DAUGHTER. – beak

LAKSHMI. – wide open. Her red –

DAUGHTER. – gullet.

LAKSHMI. Gulping everything down. Everything that does not belong to her. Every gulp reminding me of what I have had to give up. Gulp.

DAUGHTER. Gulp.

LAKSHMI. Gulp.

CLEM. What have you done?

DAUGHTER. Gulp.

LAKSHMI. Gulp.

DAUGHTER. Gulp.

LAKSHMI. Gulp.

CLEM. What have you done to the baby?

JOSH *enters*.

JOSH. I think I'm going to get a new pair of shorts at the airport.

–

Get these lily-white legs out again.

–

Don't go wild with excitement, will you?

–

Clem?

–

Clem?

CLEM. Could you love the baby if there was something wrong with –

JOSH. There's nothing wrong with the –

CLEM. Could you love it if there –

JOSH. Her. There's nothing wrong with her –

CLEM. But if –

JOSH. Stop.

CLEM. Could you though? Could you?

JOSH. For fuck's sake.

—

—

CLEM. Sorry. I'm being –

JOSH. It's okay.

CLEM. I know I'm being –

JOSH. You're worried. I understand. Let's get packed, eh?

—

—

—

CLEM. I can't breathe.

JOSH. Sit down.

CLEM. Can't breathe.

JOSH. Calm down.

CLEM. I'm suffocating. I feel like I'm –

JOSH. Sit.

—

—

Breathe.

—

—

CLEM. I'm drowning.

JOSH. Slowly.

CLEM. I'm fucking –

JOSH. Breathe.

    —

    —

    —

CLEM. My dad.

JOSH. Breathe.

CLEM. My dad.

JOSH. Breathe.

CLEM. My dad.

JOSH. No.

    —

    —

    Breathe.

    —

    —

    That's it.

    —

    —

    —

    Good girl.

    —

    —

    That's it.

—

—

—

As soon as we have our daughter, everything will make
sense. As soon as you hold her in your arms, it will all make
sense.

—

Clem?

—

Are you listening?

—

CLEM. I don't want it.

—

I don't want it any more.

JOSH. You do not get to do that. Not now. You do not get to say –

CLEM. Lakshmi tried to get rid of it. She paid three hundred
rupees to have it flushed out. She ran out of the centre, back
to her village. She found a woman who gave her a mixture of
herbs and poison and stuck a stick up her. Speared it. One of
its wings unfurled from her cunt. Black and sleek and
shining like oil. The clinic found her before she could do
anything else. They tied her hands and feet and threw her in
the car and took her back to the centre. They put her back in
the dorm with the other women who won't go near her,
because she's full of bad luck and they all know it. But it's
still in her. It's scraping her uterus, drinking her blood,
gulping her food, swelling her up with its wings, its beak
scratching at her soft insides, tap-tap-tapping on her organs.
She punches her womb every night. They have to restrain
her, tie her arms to the side of the bed, because she'll kill it if
she can. She'll kill it. And I don't blame her at all. I don't
blame her one little bit.

LAKSHMI *and* DAUGHTER *leave*.

How can I, knowing what I know?

—

Knowing what we've done.

—

Knowing what I have done to her.

Sixteen

David's House

JOSH *sits*. DAVID *in his wheelchair*. ONI *stands*.

JOSH. Please.

—

Please, David.

—

She needs you.

—

She needs you to make this alright for her.

—

David.

—

—

—

—

What are we supposed to do, just say sorry it was all a big mistake? You can keep that child because we're not interested any more. My wife has changed her mind. It's not for her after all. Terribly sorry.

—

This is our last option. Do you understand that? Our last hope and your constant bloody disapproval means…

—

If she hears it from you…

—

Everything will be okay if you could just…

ONI. Why don't you come back with Clementine another –

JOSH. We're leaving tonight.

—

You don't even have to mean it.

—

What difference does it make to you?

—

She's your daughter. She's your –

ONI. Okay. Okay…

JOSH. I'm really… She's… the stress… it's too much, it's… She's…

—

—

—

We haven't seen my brother's family for three years, because she can't bear to see the children.

—

I've taken razor blades out of her purse when her period's due.

—

I have had to spoon food into her mouth when she stopped
eating, because she couldn't see the point. For nine years,
I've watched her in so much pain and it has been unbearable.

—

Whatever you want, I'll do it. Honestly, whatever you want.

—

—

—

Fuck. Fucking hell, David, do you know what you've done?

ONI. I think it's best if you –

JOSH. What do you think about this?

—

Seriously, what do you think about him behaving like this?

—

You can't possibly think he's in the right.

ONI. I don't think anything about it.

JOSH. What is your opinion?

ONI. It's none of my business.

JOSH. But you must have some –

ONI. I don't.

JOSH. What are you? Some kind of robot? You must have –

ONI. It's not my place to –

JOSH. Yeah, but I'm asking you and –

DAVID *makes a noise.*

What?

ONI. He wants you to stop.

—

JOSH. Why should I?

—

I pay for her.

—

I pay for her to be here. And I pay for this – (*Laptop.*) and this – (*Chair.*)

—

Your aversion to money only seems relevant when it involves your daughter's happiness. You're punishing her.

ONI. Joshua, this is not –

JOSH. Is the surrogate more important to you than Clem? Is a woman you don't know more important to you than your own daughter? A woman who is thousands of miles away, who you have no connection to, who you wouldn't know existed if it wasn't for us. Do you care more about her than your own flesh –

ONI. I'm going to call Clem.

JOSH. We will change her life. For ever. We will give that woman a chance. The money will mean that she can –

DAVID *makes a noise, tries to say money.*

DAVID (*types with one finger – voice activation*). Money.

JOSH. Yes, David, money.

DAVID (*types*). Money.

JOSH. Lakshmi gets the money and we get the baby that one year ago your daughter told me she would rather be dead than live without.

DAVID (*types*). Money…

JOSH. Do you hear me? Clem wanted to die. She talked about dying. And now we're here in this nightmare. And all she

needs… I know that all she needs is to have your blessing.
To hear that it's okay from you. And you can't even –

DAVID (*types*). Money.

JOSH. I am begging you, please, for Clem. Not for me. For her.

DAVID (*types*). Money.

JOSH. Stop that.

DAVID (*types*). Money.

JOSH. Stop it.

DAVID (*types*). Money.

JOSH. You are so –

ONI. I'm going to have to –

DAVID (*types*). Money.

JOSH. All your life, the big socialist, standing up for the little
man.

ONI. It's time you left.

DAVID (*types*). Money.

JOSH. Red till you die.

ONI. This is not okay.

JOSH. And look where it's got you.

ONI. If you don't go…

DAVID (*types*). Money.

JOSH. Some shitty council house you don't even own.

ONI. I will call the police.

DAVID (*types*). Money.

JOSH. With some immigrant feeding you spaghetti hoops and
wiping your arse.

ONI. That's enough.

DAVID (*types*). Money.

JOSH. You are a husk of a man.

ONI. No.

DAVID (*types*). Money.

JOSH (*grabs the laptop*). A fucking husk of a –

ONI. Who do you think you are? Coming in here behaving like this? You people just do what you want. Trample over everything and everyone. Say what you want, take what you want. You and your wife go about your business as if it has no effect on anyone else. You don't understand anything about that country, the people, the culture. Nothing. Even the change of the law is brushed aside as if it's been put in place to inconvenience you. You have no idea what you are involved in. No. Worse than that, you don't care. You just close your eyes to it. You and your stupid wife. Wake up. Wake up, you stupid stupid people.

—

JOSH. Jesus.

JOSH *bursts out laughing. They watch him. He stops.*

—

—

(*To* ONI.) What do you think will happen to a baby girl in India that nobody wants?

—

Well?

—

What's going to be the story for that baby? Another unwanted mouth to feed.

—

Another unwanted girl.

—

A girl with no genetic link to the woman who bears her? Do you think that's going to end well?

ONI. That isn't going to happen.

JOSH. Isn't it?

ONI. You are going to get that baby girl and you are going to bring her home.

JOSH. Well the government isn't making that easy for me and my wife is no longer –

ONI. You have started something and you have to finish it.

—

You have a duty of care to that child.

—

That child needs you.

—

JOSH. I never wanted this.

—

I did it because she...

—

She was the one who...

ONI. You are the father.

—

You must feel some kind of... You are her father.

—

You are going to go to India and get your daughter.

JOSH. Am I?

ONI. Yes.

JOSH. Not without my wife, I'm not.

—

I'm not going anywhere without my wife.

—

CLEM *walks in.*

CLEM. Dad?

JOSH. What are you doing here?

CLEM. What's happened to the birds?

JOSH. What are you –

CLEM. What's happened to the –

JOSH. Is everything –

CLEM. The finches. What's happened to –

ONI. They've gone.

—

Evka left the aviary door open. She was feeding them and David had a fall. She heard him. She panicked and she ran into the house. The birds flew out.

CLEM. When?

ONI. Three weeks ago.

CLEM. Why didn't you tell me?

—

I could have done something. I could have –

ONI. What? What could you have done?

—

—

CLEM. I'll get you some more. We'll get –

DAVID *makes a noise*.

But –

DAVID *makes a noise*.

I can get –

ONI. He does not want any more.

CLEM. But he loves the finches.

—

The birds are…

—

Daddy, you love those finches.

—

—

I'm sorry.

—

—

—

She goes towards DAVID. JOSH *reaches for her. She pushes him away. She sits on the floor at* DAVID*'s feet*.

—

—

I am so so sorry.

—

—

—

She puts her head on DAVID*'s knee*. DAVID *stares ahead. She cries*.

—

—

—

—

—

—

—

JOSH *looks at* ONI. *She looks back at him.*

—

—

—

—

—

—

—

—

—

—

—

—

—

ONI. Clementine…

—

David wanted me to tell you something.

—

He asked me to…

—

He wanted me to tell you he was wrong.

—

—

He judged too harshly.

—

He thinks…

—

He thinks you will be a very good mother.

—

—

—

—

—

—

—

—

—

—

—

Seventeen

DAVID *is in front of the television. Unable to move. A new*
CARER *sits reading a magazine.*

LAKSHMI *outside the clinic. Milk seeps from her breasts. She*
holds a paper bag of money. She blinks against the sunlight.

A hotel room. JOSH *sits in a chair holding a newborn baby.*
CLEM *comes out of the bathroom. She hands him a bottle of*
milk. He looks at her. He stands up and hands her the baby.
A moment. She takes the baby and sits down. She feeds her.
She looks out.

A small Indian GIRL *dances on a table. A piece of string round*
her wrist. She is wearing make-up. Far too old for her.

The End.

Other Titles in this Series

'A great published script makes you understand what the play is, at its heart' *Slate Magazine*

Enjoyed this book? Choose from hundreds more classic and contemporary plays from Nick Hern Books, the UK's leading independent theatre publisher.

Our full range is available to browse online now, including:

Award-winning plays from leading contemporary dramatists, including *King Charles III* by Mike Bartlett, *Anne Boleyn* by Howard Brenton, *Jerusalem* by Jez Butterworth, *A Breakfast of Eels* by Robert Holman, *Chimerica* by Lucy Kirkwood, *The Night Alive* by Conor McPherson, *The James Plays* by Rona Munro, *Nell Gwynn* by Jessica Swale, and many more…

Ground-breaking drama from the most exciting up-and-coming playwrights, including Vivienne Franzmann, James Fritz, Ella Hickson, Anna Jordan, Jack Thorne, Phoebe Waller-Bridge, Tom Wells, and many more…

Twentieth-century classics, including *Cloud Nine* by Caryl Churchill, *Death and the Maiden* by Ariel Dorfman, *Pentecost* by David Edgar, *Angels in America* by Tony Kushner, *Long Day's Journey into Night* by Eugene O'Neill, *The Deep Blue Sea* by Terence Rattigan, *Machinal* by Sophie Treadwell, and many more…

Timeless masterpieces from playwrights throughout the ages, including Anton Chekhov, Euripides, Henrik Ibsen, Federico García Lorca, Christopher Marlowe, Molière, William Shakespeare, Richard Brinsley Sheridan, Oscar Wilde, and many more…

Every playscript is a world waiting to be explored. Find yours at **www.nickhernbooks.co.uk** – you'll receive a 20% discount, plus free UK postage & packaging for orders over £30.

'Publishing plays gives permanent form to an evanescent art, and allows many more people to have some kind of experience of a play than could ever see it in the theatre' *Nick Hern, publisher*

www.nickhernbooks.co.uk

A Nick Hern Book

Bodies first published in Great Britain in 2017 as a paperback original by Nick Hern Books Limited, The Glasshouse, 49a Goldhawk Road, London W12 8QP, in association with the Royal Court Theatre, London

Bodies copyright © 2017 Vivienne Franzmann

Vivienne Franzmann has asserted her right to be identified as the author of this work

Cover design by Root

Designed and typeset by Nick Hern Books, London
Printed in Great Britain by CPI Group (UK) Ltd

A CIP catalogue record for this book is available from the British Library

ISBN 978 1 84842 659 7